The 5S's

Five Keys to a
Total Quality Environment

The
5S's

Five Keys to a
Total Quality Environment

Takashi Osada

Asian Productivity Organization

Published in 1991 by
  Asian Productivity Organization
  4-14, Akasaka 8-chome
  Minato-ku, Tokyo 107
  Japan

Distributed in North America, the United Kingdom, and Western Europe by
  Quality Resources
  A Division of The Kraus Organization Limited
  One Water Street
  White Plains, NY 10601

Originally published in Japanese under the title *5S—Tezukuri no Manejimento
Shuho* by Japan Institute of Plant Maintenance, Tokyo, Japan. Copyright ©
1989 by T. Osada. All rights reserved. This is an authorized English lan-
guage translation from the Japanese edition under arrangement with Japan
Institute of Plant Maintenance.

ISBN 92-833-1116-7 (Paper)
ISBN 92-833-1115-9 (Cloth)

Cover design by Joseph DePinho.

Printed in Hong Kong by Nordica International Ltd.
Eighth Printing 1998

Contents

Introduction

Japanese industry did not start off strong. In fact, Japanese industry has very little comparative advantage as comparative advantage has traditionally been understood. There is no oil gushing out of the ground. There are no vast mines reaping with iron ore. The coal veins are poor and uneconomical. The forests are scraggly. The country cannot even grow enough food to feed its people.

Then why is Japanese industry considered such a threat in so many lands? Because there is one resource that Japan does have in abundance: people who know that nothing comes free and who are willing to study hard and work hard to earn their way. Japan's functional illiteracy rate is among the lowest in the world. Its labor relations are among the most harmonious because workers know the importance of finding better ways of doing things to make their jobs easier, their output better, and their lives more comfortable.

Best known overseas are such cooperative efforts as quality circles organized at the shop level to give workers the analytical tools, management information, and authority they need to make improvements in the way things are done. At the better companies, these quality circles spread all the way through the company, from top to bottom, in concerted programs of total quality control (TQC). In addition, there are also *kaizen*, just-in-time manufacturing, and a host of other techniques for involving everyone in turning out better products.

Yet even the quality control (QC) circles that seem basic are not the first step. The first step has to be the 5S movement with its emphasis on a clean, well-organized workplace. Without this emphasis, it is impossible to tell where the problems are. Without well-defined and consistently followed operating procedures, it is impossible to tell what you are doing right or wrong. Without the 5S movement, none of the other campaigns and innovations that have been invented for better working conditions and superior products will be to any avail.

What is the 5S movement? Basically, it is a determination to organize the workplace, to keep it neat, to clean, to maintain standardized conditions, and to maintain the discipline that is needed to do a good job. The name 5S comes from the first letters of the five Japanese terms, *seiri, seiton, seiso, seiketsu,* and *shitsuke,* that are its dictums. Because these terms are perhaps a little much for non-Japanese to remember, they have been translated here as organization, neatness, cleaning, standardization, and discipline. Unfortunately, ONCSD is not as nearly elegant as 5S, and the package is thus referred to as the 5S's in this book. As the Japanese and English terms have some overlapping areas of meaning, you will find that they have sometimes been translated differently in the English texts available today. We have included the Japanese term at the beginning of the chapter in which it is covered, to help clarify which aspect of the 5S system is being discussed.

As explained in the following ten chapters, the 5S's are not that difficult to understand. However, they are very difficult to do well. They require perseverance and determination. They require constant effort. They require the ability to see what is important and to pay attention to details. They may not show dramatic results, but they do show results. They show results in terms of more convenient work practices. They show results in terms of less downtime. They show results in terms of workers who take pride in their work. And they show results in higher productivity and better quality because people who care about their work do a better job.

It is important, however, that this be a total companywide effort. You cannot simply tell the factory workers to implement the 5S's. Management also has to do its part. The 5S's have to be practices at the office as well as at the factory. Management has to be 100% behind the campaign. Everyone has to do his or her part. It will not be easy, but it will be rewarding.

After explaining the basic thinking behind the 5S campaign and the reasons why every workplace can benefit from the 5S's, the book discusses each of the five in detail. Finally, it looks at the 5S's in the office and management's role. Every effort has been made to keep this work approachable to everyone and to avoid the kind of technical jargon that permeates so much management writing. The 5S's are for everyone, not just for a few experts.

March 1991   Takashi Osada

Chapter 1

The 5S Revolution

1.1. EVERYBODY HAS TO PITCH IN

Know what you're supposed to do and do it. Management magazines have carried considerable discussions about the relative merits of top–down vs. bottom–up management, but to ask this question is to miss the point. Top–down management doesn't work if the people on the receiving end of the orders do not dance to management's tune. And it is impossible to get the full benefits of bottom–up management unless the people at the top are committed to making it work.

Business is very much a team sport. Some people are managers, some are players, and some are support—but they all have to do their jobs if the team expects to win. On the best teams, each person knows what his job is and does it.

The synergetic (or cooperative) effect. This effect means the really good teams do not have any standout stars. In baseball, for example, if the fielding is good, the batters, rather than all trying to be home-run hitters, are glad to just go for bunts, sacrifice flies, and run the bases as hard as they can. It is the combination of all of these little things that makes a winning team. The really good team is more than the sum of its players. On an ordinary team, one plus one is two, but on the best team it is three. Rather than having one star, the whole team stars. However, in business just as in sports, it is possible for one plus one to be one—or even less than one—if the players are working at cross purposes and undercutting each other.

That is why so many Japanese companies, large and small, are working so hard to promote total participation quality activities that involve everyone in a team effort. But, as the paucity of results demonstrates, this is not an easy thing to do.

This is where the 5S movement comes in. Not only is the 5S movement indispensable to involving everyone, it is also an activity in which major progress is readily attainable.

1.2. THE DIFFICULT THINGS ARE EASY, BUT THE EASY THINGS ELUDE YOU

Why can't you make a concerted effort?   If you take a walk around Japanese industry, you will see lots of signs exhorting people to work on the 5S's or at least to work on the first three (organization, neatness, and cleaning). But because these exhortations are uniformly visible does not mean that all companies are getting uniformly good results. The 5S's seem so easy to understand, and so easy to do. Then why are they so difficult?

They're so difficult because they look so easy—because everybody assumes they're going to be a snap—and so nobody really works at them. They're so difficult because people don't understand what the 5S's are all about. Setting up an operation and establishing the parameters, for example, are impossible unless you really know the work inside out and have had lots of practice.

If you can't do the 5S's, you can't do the other work.
Although most work is done by following standard operating
procedures (SOPs), it is impossible for someone else to tell
whether or not the work was really being done to SOPs. The
only way to tell is to measure the finished project and see if it
meets the job specifications. If it does—if it is within acceptable
tolerance levels—it is assumed that the job was done according
to SOPs. But it may well be that the inspection procedures and
measurement equipment were off. Unless the measurement
devices and other inspection tools are kept in impeccable condition, they will be useless and there will be no way at all of
knowing if the job has been done to SOPs.

In a very real way, it might be said that not only does
failure to ensure that the measurement and other inspection
equipment is kept in tip-top condition make it impossible to
tell if the job has been done right, the fact that a company is
unable to keep its measurement and inspection equipment in
good condition suggests that it is also unable to keep its other
equipment and operating procedures in good condition and
unable to do the job right.

The most difficult operating procedures have to start with
the 5S's. Even though the 5S's look like little things—like easy
things—it is important that they not be slighted and that everyone pitch in to do them.

1.3. THE COMPANY THAT'S DOING BADLY
IS DOING THE 5S's BADLY

Features common to nonperforming workplaces. If you
take the time to look at some of the nonperforming workplaces
where things are not done right, you will notice that there are
a number of things they all have in common.

For example, the interpersonal relations are usually bad.
People do not say hello to each other. The people look worn
out. There is a high absenteeism rate. The workers don't make
suggestions on how to improve the work processes and don't
seem to care about their work. The QC circle activities are stale-

mated. The line is beset with defectives and reworking. And more. On the line, the equipment is dirty instead of clean, tools are lying around instead of in their proper places, and there are confusing mountains of rejects and parts. In short, the place is a mess.

The 5S's are your first indicator.   Likewise, when the 5S's go bad, it usually means that there is something more fundamentally wrong. In that sense, the 5S's are your first indicator of how well things are going. When the 5S's are being implemented, things are going well. When they're not, you're in trouble. But this does not just mean that things are going badly because the 5S's are not being observed. Rather, it means that you have delivery, quality, or other problems in addition, that these problems have poisoned the interpersonal relations, and that the 5S's are being neglected as a result. So the state of your 5S activities is both cause and result.

It is difficult for an outsider to see exactly how things are on the shop floor, but the 5S's will give you an accurate picture every time.

1.4. FROM CORRECTION TO PREVENTION

Busy just putting things right.   When you watch management in action, you will notice that they spend a lot of their time just going back and trying to put things right. They are reacting to trouble after the fact. Yet when you look at the kinds of problems they are reacting to, it is clear that the causes of these problems are usually simple things. They are little things that nobody noticed. They are the sorts of problems that could have been taken care of in 30 minutes if you had noticed them early on, but that take 3 days to rectify afterward.

Why does this happen with such disconcerting frequency? It has been said that an ounce of prevention is worth a pound of cure, that complacency is the enemy, and that a single match can burn down a whole town. That is why the fire department does not just tell people to be careful not to start fires. It tells them to be sure that match is out. Fire prevention starts not with general principles, but with simple specifics.

Incessantly reacting to problems after the fact is like seeing the fire without seeing the tinder or seeing the first spark. The fire is a problem, of course, but it would not have happened if the spark and the tinder had not been neglected for so long. And just pointing out the fire is no good unless you also correct the circumstances that caused it.

Moving from managing by results to managing by causes. Yet all of us are all too prone to look at the results and judge by results. Instead, we need to look at the causes. We need to look at the process. If the process is right, the results will take care of themselves.

1.5. NOT NOTICING THAT THE BASICS ARE BEING IGNORED

In trying to produce quality products, we set necessary conditions and facilitating conditions, and we know full well that both sets have to be met if we expect to do a good job. Management, line workers, and everybody else knows this, and everybody works to see that things are managed right on a daily basis and that improvements are made.

Emphasizing the basics. But there is one more set of conditions that has to be satisfied. This is the set of basic conditions. They are little things like making sure that the oil you use is free of impurities and that bolts are tightened properly. Little, but basic.

Of course, neglecting these things is not going to result in defectives right away. It will be a while. But time will tell. After a while, you will notice that things are going wrong, that things are not turning out the way they're supposed to. For example, if you don't have enough oil in the machinery, or if what is there is dirty, you'll notice that things stick. You'll notice that residue on sliding parts results in friction and heating. You'll notice that the equipment starts to rattle and some of the attachments may even fall off because a bolt was not tightened right a long time ago. And you'll notice that you end up with a higher defect rate and lax management. These things tend to snowball unless they are caught early on.

It's important to realize that it's important. But because these things don't lead to problems right away, people tend to forget how important they are. There is no sense of urgency, and so they get put off. Things are "close enough" rather than "right." Even though these are little things and could easily be taken care of as part of the everyday routine, they get neglected because they are so familiar.

But when trouble erupts, management is running frantically all over the place trying to put out one fire after another. They are in a panic, treating the symptoms, and they don't have time to look at the underlying causes. They look for someone to blame instead of a cause to fix.

If they really want to get to the heart of the problem, they would take a long and hard look at the incongruities in the operating procedures and the pervasive climate that allows people to ignore the SOPs. They would work on making sure everybody knows what to do and does it. They would enhance their operational control of the processes. These sound like little things, but they're not. They're basic and they're paramount.

Hotbeds of inefficiency. When you look at all the ways people are "saving time" by ignoring the basics, it is clear that the workshop is more often than not a hotbed of inefficiency.

There is so much that has to be done. There is so much that the 5S's can do for you. Just look around. There are all kinds of situations where a little time spent on the 5S's today can save you all kinds of time later. Equipment that you just know is going to start turning out defectives someday. Inspection equipment that is so dirty you can't bear to look at it. Fire extinguishers that are still sitting around long past the refill deadline. Tool boxes that you can't find right away. And even equipment that you want to have fixed but can't because it is so dirty. A little time with the 5S's now can yield tremendous savings in terms of quality, accident prevention, productivity, and in every other way.

1.6. THE HUMAN DIFFERENCE

Using their heads to live longer. There are all kinds of animals headed for extinction, but the human population just keeps on growing and our lifespan gets longer and longer. Although it goes without saying that this is due to the advances of medical science, that alone is not the answer, for medical science itself has advanced because people think things through, put their heads together, and work on making their environment more conducive to human life. People are careful not to get sick or have accidents.

They wash their hands. They clean. They install running water and sewer systems. They see that their garbage is taken care of instead of left lying around. They sterilize and pasteurize. They are careful about what they eat and what they do. And the sum of all of these efforts is what we call civilization.

The 5S's as crime prevention? In effect, it is the 5S's that separate people from animals. People make an effort to keep their homes bright and clean and try to create and maintain good interpersonal relations at work. They build dams and windbreaks to prevent erosion. They keep things orderly, and that makes it easier to tell when something is amiss. Just as sloth and filth breed accidents at work, so do they breed crime in our cities. Little wonder it has been suggested that you can tell a city where the 5S's are not being observed just by looking at the crime rate. Little wonder there are 5S cities such as Singapore where littering draws a stiff fine.

1.7. THE 5S's AT HOME AND AT WORK

The same smarts at home and at work. There are all kinds of habits and little things we do in ordinary life to make our lives go more smoothly. These are what might be called our everyday-life smarts. For example, we say hello to people. We wash our hands before meals. We brush our teeth. We are in the habit of cleaning up right after every meal. We know where our knives, spoons, and forks go. We clean the house. We have aprons, handkerchiefs, towels, brooms, and other things to help us keep things clean. We have accumulated a wealth of good habits and useful innovations related to hygiene. We have gutters and eaves on the roof to channel the rainwater so it doesn't splash everyone. We take pains to keep the ventilation good so the flooring and beams of the house don't rot. And we hang the bedding out to the sun when we can.

When you think about it, you'll realize that these are all 5S practices. Washing the dishes right after we eat and cleaning things as soon as they get dirty are easy. But it is much more of a bother if you let them sit and let the grime harden. This is worth remembering.

The 5S's are preparations to keep things in tip-top shape. These good habits carry over into the workplace as well. The 5S's are actually what you do to ensure that you will be able to do your job at peak efficiency. They are improvements in the way you take care of things so that you don't have to waste a lot of time looking for them. It is just like knowing where your knife and fork will be when you want them.

Just like the way you take care of your tableware at the house and your tools at work—just like the way you put away your winter clothes and put on your summer clothes when the weather becomes hot—these are things that you do so that your tools will always be in tip-top shape when you need them.

1.8. WHY ACCIDENTS HAPPEN WITH EVEN THE MOST SOPHISTICATED SYSTEMS

There has been a spate of accidents with some of the most sophisticated engineering feats in history—accidents at nuclear power plants, explosion of the space shuttle, airplane crashes and computer system crashes, and telecommunications systems that shut down. Yet when the causes of the accidents are analyzed, more likely than not they are found at the interfaces of the equipment and the operators. People made an operational mistake, the repairs were not done properly, and other human error is to blame in most cases. And even if it is just one person's mistake, the results can be disastrous with today's sophisticated systems.

If the truth be told, many of today's systems are perhaps too sophisticated and too complex. They are better than the people that run them. And because most people are no longer able to understand the systems' intricacies, it is no wonder that they depend too much on the systems themselves and have given up trying to control them.

The same is true in the modern factory or office. Robots, for example, can be very useful and productive if they are used right, but they can also be extremely destructive if used wrongly. In effect, the greater the advantages to our sophisticated and complex systems, the greater the danger that a careless mistake will bring disaster.

People are unable to sustain long-term tension.   Too often, we forget that people are unable to sustain a high level of concentration at very complex tasks for very long periods of time. That is why it is important that we remember that people are accident-prone and tend to make mistakes. Once we remember this, our outlook will change.

The future is in increasing factory automation and increasingly complex systems, and it is important that we learn how to cope with this situation. We need to go back to the beginning and take a fresh look at this issue. And when we do, we will find that we need to start with the 5S's.

1.9. THE NEED TO AVOID HUMAN ERROR

What happens when the 5S's are wrong on sophisticated equipment?   No matter how sophisticated a system you are working with—no matter how advanced the technology is— you are going to have problems if the control panel is dirty or the gauges are covered with grime. In the factory, no matter how good the operating instructions are, you are going to have trouble if people keep dropping things, if the workplace is filthy with grime and oil from the machinery, and if the equipment was last cleaned who knows when. You are not going to be able to maintain quality with that kind of a situation, nor are you going to be able to maintain the equipment for long.

No matter how good the intentions or the equipment, it is people who have to put the intentions into practice and operate the equipment. And that means that the more advanced the equipment, the more modern human attitudes have to be.

Improving the quality of human behavior.   That means you have to improve the quality of human behavior for each and every person. For example, if someone tells a computer to do the wrong thing or inputs improper data, the computer will not know the difference and will follow instructions exactly. That is why it is so important that your people do the right thing.

That is why it so important that a mind-set be established in each and every person so he or she thinks about and mentally checks every action. Because that is the only way you are going to prevent simple but disastrous errors such as inputting the wrong number, misreading a figure, attaching a part incorrectly, forgetting to check something, or letting something go ''just this once.''

1.10.   DOES EVERYBODY FOLLOW INSTRUCTIONS?

Conveying instructions accurately.   There are more and more supervisors and other management people today wondering why everybody doesn't follow instructions and do what they're supposed to. Yet when you investigate these cases, you often find that the instructions were not conveyed accurately and concisely to start with. People rely upon words and a variety of other communication tools to get their message across, but communication is actually a very difficult art.

There was, for example, the case of a Japanese trying to communicate operating procedures at a factory in the United States. The workers kept saying, "Yeah, I gotcha." But they didn't follow instructions. So the supervisor tried once more. This time, he got, "I see," but still the workers kept on doing things wrong. So he tried once again. And this time, the workers said, "I understand." But even so, the procedures were not followed. Finally, after yet another explanation, the response was, "I agree," and this time the workers followed the right procedure because they finally understood what it was all about.

Active vs. passive agreement. This is not simply a cross-cultural problem. The same thing happens in Japan as well. Someone can say "Hai" until he is blue in the face, but that doesn't mean he has really understood you. It may simply mean "I hear you talking." As such, it is very much like the English "I see." And it is essential that the instructor, supervisor, or whoever get beyond that stage to the "I understand" stage and then finally to the "I agree" stage. The person saying "Hai," "Yeah," or whatever is using these terms to indicate different degrees of understanding, and it is essential that the person who is explaining something be able to understand what level of understanding is being achieved.

More often than not, when people do not do what they are told, it is because they did not fully understand what they were told to do. They may have understood the whats, but they did not understand the whys, and so the conformance is only begrudging at best. That is why it is important to get up to the "I agree" level of understanding.

Here, too, the 5S's can help by making sure that everyone understands at the highest level.

SUMMARY

- The 5S's have been around a long time, and there is nothing new about them. We just have not been that aware of them until now. So when we look around, there is a lot of room for improvement.

- When you look at why we need the 5S's at work, it is immediately clear that there are many things that we do without thinking. The 5S's can help in everything we do.

- The 5S's are like a mirror reflecting our attitudes and behavioral patterns. Even so, we all too often avert our eyes and prefer not to look at what we see there.

- Many of the everyday problems that we encounter would be cleared up if only we paid more attention to the 5S's. Not observing the 5S's is a mark of a lazy mind and a slothful attitude.

- Before management and supervisors tell other people they have to implement the 5S's, they need to take a good look at things and see if they really understand why themselves.

Chapter 2

What a Difference the 5S's Make

2.1. ONGOING MANAGEMENT MAKES THE BEST WORKPLACE: TWO PATTERNS FOR IMPROVEMENT

Kaizen (continuous improvement) and *kaizen* management are all the rage in business circles today, but it all too often happens that management is so busy chasing after this or that rainbow that it comes up with a pot of nothing.

Factories make a great show of competing for worker suggestions, but all too often it happens that management ends up with a lot of marginally useful suggestions that have only marginal effect. It is enough to make you wonder if anybody is really taking the suggestion system seriously. Even when the suggestions are excellent, the results leave something to be desired.

And even at companies where they do not spend a lot of time talking about this or that management method or *kaizen*, it is clear from just one look at the factory floor that everybody is working together and that this is a good company.

Silver-bullet improvements.   Basically, there are two ways to make improvements. One is what might be called the silver-bullet method. This is a massive overhaul that roots out all the problems and puts everything right in one fell swoop. For example, if you have a machine that has repeated problems with the limit switches, you might decide to pull out the old switch mechanism and install a new one. If you are encountering a lot of breakage, you might decide to switch to stronger materials. Of if you are getting a lot of friction, you might decide to spend more on surface-treatment technology. All of these are one-shot silver-bullet solutions. They take a lot of technical expertise, but a few good engineers can do wonders for the factory this way.

Once the engineers have made the improvements, they typically draw up tool-change procedures, inspection procedures, oiling procedures, and other checklists on how to keep the equipment operating at the higher level. But if the people ignore these checklists, all of the improvements will be for naught and all of the effort will have been wasted. Thus, workers must spend most of their time just maintaining checklists and keeping things working the way they are supposed to.

And the company that cannot do this deserves to go belly up. There are companies like that. They implement great improvements, and then they revert back to their old ways and things are worse than before. These are the companies that you read about in the business obituary column.

In fact, whether or not the workers will be able to maintain the improvements and keep things working right depends on how aware the workers are of their importance. Do they know that they are just as much management as management is? The 5S's are crucial here.

The gradualist approach.   When you are not feeling well, you may have to take medicine to get back on track. But it is even more important that you have good habits to stay fit. Get lots of sleep. Exercise. Eat the right foods. The proper habits, like the ancient Chinese herbal remedies, are long-term cures to keep you in good health. And this is the second type of improvement.

The 5S's are the first step toward a long-term program of good health for your company.

2.2. THE 5S's ARE THE MANAGEMENT BAROMETER: WELL-RUN FACTORIES ARE WELL RUN BY EVERYONE

If you take the time to look at different factories, you will find that there are many factories where everybody seems to be angry at the world or where it is hard to tell exactly what is happening. But on the other hand, you will also find that there are many factories where things are immaculate and well-ordered (even if nobody says anything about the 5S's) and where everybody is working together as a team, doing work they take pride in.

If you can do the 5S's, you can do anything.   Although the 5S's can be most effective in improving the management of any factory, there are also a number of other activities being promoted to forge better work teams and to improve working conditions. Yet if you can do the 5S's, you can also implement the other systems with no problems and to good effect. The reason for this is that the 5S's do not require a lot of fancy managerial staff. Instead, they depend on each and every worker to implement them and to self-manage for maximum effect. The 5S's cannot succeed unless everyone is on board and thinking about it. But if they are, the other systems are already half-implemented.

In the process of formulating and implementing the 5S standards, the managerial level at the plant will become obvious. In some cases, it will be encouraging. But in other cases it will be disappointing—because just as the company that can do well with the 5S's can also do well with the other systems, the company that cannot even implement the basic 5S's will not be able to do any of the other things that management wants it to.

Studying management basics with the 5S's.   What is management for? Very simply, it is to devise easy-to-follow procedures, to make sure that everything is operating right, to get everyone involved in making and maintaining improvements, to improve the level of operations, and, hence, to improve the quality assurance level. Seen this way, it should be clear that it is possible to study management basics with the 5S's.

The 5S's are the easiest principles there are to understand. They lend themselves to total participation. There are no gains unless the 5S's are implemented, but the gains that are achieved from implementation are clear for everyone to see. In fact, the 5S's are the prototype total participation program. The 5S's are the embodiment of total participation joy and total participation know-how. Thus, it has been said that the 5S's are a barometer telling you how well a company is managed and a lodestone telling you how total worker participation is.

2.3. THE FACTORY AS A SALES TOOL

Companies that can be proud of their factories.   Manufacturers are companies that make products and then sell them, and they survive on the profits that they make from selling their wares. For the manufacturer, the factory is an asset. And it should be an asset that the manufacturer can be proud of.

It is not enough that the finished product feature high quality and low cost. It is also essential that the process that produced the product—meaning the factory—feature outstanding technology and management.

If you go to a food processing plant and it is filthy, or if you go to a plant where precision tools are made and the shop floor is dirty and there are filings lying in pools of grease, it doesn't matter how nice the finished product looks or how glib the salesmen are. There is a sense of foreboding and a fear that you would be better off not dealing with this company. The factory is the reality, and you tend to trust your judgment of it more than your impressions of the product.

When the salesmen carry pictures of the factory.   Yet the impression that the factory makes does not sell the product directly. Rather, it sells the idea that the company is well-managed and that it will be able to sustain a consistent level of quality. This is, in fact, the best thing that factory workers can do to contribute to the sales effort.

There is one company where the salesmen carry photos of the factory, and part of their pitch includes an invitation to would-be customers to come and visit the plant. This is a powerful sales tool, for it indicates complete confidence in the process behind the product.

2.4. THE 5S's AS BEHAVIORAL SCIENCE

Over the past few years, there have been more and more popular workshops on walking rallies and other methods of getting people moving and involved in what they are doing.

The 5S's also operate on this "actions speak louder than words" principle. The most effective way to get things done is not to expound on how things ought to be, but to take a hard look at the realities and then to make the changes on the actual factory floor. The way to wake up everyone is to have everyone take part, to create a sense of participation and group identity, and to create a sense of wonder and accomplishment. There are reasons why it has been said that one picture is worth a thousand words and that seeing is believing.

No shortcut to the 5S's, only a lot of elbow grease.   People are very bookish these days. They know all of the arguments. They know all of the theories. They know exactly what has to be done. But they also know all the reasons why it cannot be done, and they will set these out in great detail. The result is that things don't get done. Somehow, they seem to feel that just because they know what has to be done, they can do it anytime and it does not have to be done now. Somehow, they seem to feel that knowing is a substitute for doing. So they never get down to work and things just go from bad to worse.

At times like this, it is crucial that a start be made. It can and maybe even should be made with something simple. This is where the 5S's come in. The theory behind them is not all that difficult. But the theory doesn't mean anything unless it is accompanied by the practice. The important thing is to start now. Get your hands dirty. Find the problems. And fix them. (See Figure 2.1.)

It is only by actually practicing the 5S's that you are really going to understand them. There is no easy road to understanding. There are no shortcuts. There is only hard work. The only understanding comes from doing.

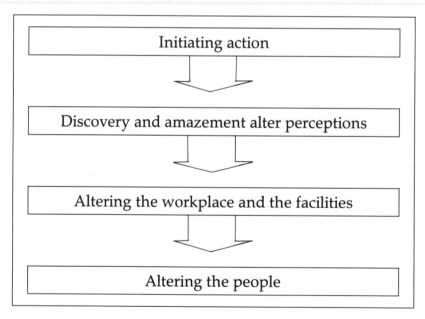

FIGURE 2.1.

2.5. USING THE FACTORY EXPERIENCE
TO CLEANSE THE HEART

Almost everyone in Japan goes on a cleaning binge at the end of the year. They want to get ready for the new year in style. They want to get off to a clean start. So they sweep out the dirt in the corners. They dust the high places. And they try to purify their spirits as well. Thus, this tradition of year-end cleaning is seen as a great virtue in Japan.

Cleaning as a way of purifying the spirit. This cleaning is the basis of education. The rawest novice at the temple starts by being assigned to cleaning duty. The apprentice who wants to learn a craftsman's trade starts by cleaning. The scientist is first assigned to clean the lab. People learning the martial arts or the performing arts also start by learning the cleaning arts.

Even before they begin producing anything, the ritual of cleaning ensures that they are worthy of their work. As such, cleaning is as much to purify the heart as it is to clean the external trappings.

Changing both thinking and behavior. Recently, both the school and the home have abandoned their responsibilities in Japan. Instead, people now learn the basis of all social behavior at the workplace with on-the-job training. The basis for this attitude is to treat all things carefully. The more careful and attentive someone is about inspecting the machinery at the factory, the more likely he or she is to notice little things on a daily basis. The more likely he or she is to care for the equipment and use it carefully. This is when people are at their best, when they can see the situation clearly, and when they are concerned for their fellow workers and try to do a better job. This is the first step to a pure heart.

When people have this experience in their work, when they come together with their fellow workers and develop the spirit of working together, this also changes their attitude, their manner of thinking, and the way they act. So the factory is not simply a place for making things. It is also a place for making people better.

2.6. A SYSTEM THAT ENCOURAGES RESPONSIBLE BEHAVIOR

Different responsibilities for management and worker. If we divide responsibility into management responsibility and worker responsibility from the standpoint of the work, it is clear that the two are different. Management has to take responsibility for the finished product, of course, but the worker has quite a different kind of responsibility.

For example, one of the prerequisites to avoiding equipment failure is that the machinery be oiled without fail. But the worker is not responsible for seeing that the machine does not develop any problems. The worker is only responsible for oiling it regularly and without fail. In effect, the worker is not responsible for the result, but for the process. It is the process that leads to the result, and it is the worker who is responsible for the process.

That is why the best way to prevent problems is for every worker to state clearly what processes he or she is responsible for and then to fulfill these responsibilities as best he or she can each and every day.

The importance of individual responsibility. Management that simply draws up regulations and insists on their being followed is not going to last long. Instead, you need a sense of people working together and helping each other, each person taking the extra time and initiative to do a good job, and each person being very conscious of what he or she is doing and why. You need responsible behavior—responsible behavior by each and every worker on an individual basis.

2.7. THE 5S's AS A MANAGEMENT PHILOSOPHY

The new concept of the 5S's. The times demand a new concept of the 5S's. Processing and assembly plants that use a lot of grease are reborn as "living-room factories." Other factories are emerging as "clean-room factories," rivaling even the most spotless laboratory. And people have taken to referring to the factory as the "showroom."

On the employment side, it is becoming increasingly difficult for manufacturing companies that have dirty plants to attract the workers they need. Conversely, companies that have clean factories are organizing factory tours for their employees' families and even for their customers.

The 5S's as a management technique. Until recently, the 5S's were a minor movement on the fringes of productivity and production. They were nice, but not essential. Now, however, management is changing its tune and realizing that the 5S's are central to its thinking and its management philosophy. It is coming to see that the 5S's are a key management technique.

More and more Euro-American companies have tried to adopt Japanese management in recent years. And they are realizing that the 5S's are an essential part of this management.

One U.S. plant, for example, mounted a major housekeeping campaign. This was revolutionary, as was the campaign's slogan: Good housekeeping is up to you.

In Japan, top corporate executives have cited the 5S's as their number one management priority. Of course, the term 5S's is used here in the broadest sense. There are, after all, executives who refer to the 4S's + 1. There are executives who talk of the 6S's. And there are other variations on this theme. But it is the 5S's that are basic.

2.8. THE 5S's AS THE ULTIMATE PURSUIT OF PRODUCTIVITY: THE EMERGENCE OF THE NEW 5S's

The new 5S's for productivity and quality. There is a 5S revolution underway for greater productivity and quality in the electronics, medical equipment, precision processing, assembly, and the rest of Japan's cutting-edge industries.

People have come to sense the limits to the old superficial 5S campaigns centered on organization and neatness. They have come to realize that the need for unparalleled quality demands the elimination of even minute contamination (as expressed in the clean rooms and the degrees of cleanness). They have come to realize that they need to control not only grime, but even static electricity, temperature, and humidity. They have come to realize that they need to eliminate errors at the micromillimeter level if they want top quality. They are thus questing for new levels of cleanliness, combining management philosophy and the latest technology. In short, they are striving for the 5S's as they should be.

The transformed workplace.   And as a result, everything has been changed. People have, for example, abandoned the old metallic grays that do not show the dirt and adopted new spotless white. White is all over the Japanese factory today—on the machinery, the interiors, the buildings, and even the workers' uniforms. There is a new emphasis on being clean and competitive.

SUMMARY

- Although the 5S movement obviously results in major improvements in 5S areas, it is even more important in changing the way people approach their work and what they do. It is crucial in enabling people to see things more clearly.
- It is impossible to mount a 5S campaign with just one or two people. You need to have everyone actively involved. Each of the individual things that needs to be done is simple enough in itself. The difficult thing is to keep doing them. This requires determination, persistence, and cooperation. But that combination in turn creates a new sense of team identity and a better corporate climate.
- It is important to start by doing. No matter how well you understand the theory, the theory does not produce results. Only doing does. And this doing has the power to change the way people look at things. It has the power to transform them. It is thus akin to the Zen training that novice priests undergo. It is management in the best sense.

• Every part of the 5S process is important. Every step has the potential for opening our eyes. The 5S's are the best way there is to eliminate waste. That is why the 5S's have been adopted in the electronics and precision machinery industries at the technological forefront. That is why there is a new 5S awareness emerging.

Chapter 3

Meaning and Purposes of the 5S's

3.1. MEANING OF THE 5S's

In the last analysis, the 5S's are intended to eliminate waste. Just as every word has its broader interpretation, so do the 5S activities have their broader and somewhat vague sense. Thus, it is important here to clarify exactly what the 5S's are, where they are intended to get you, and how the 5S activities should be structured to get you there. What exactly are the 5S's and what can they do for you?

Seiri = Organization

In general usage, this means to put things in order—to organize them—in accordance with specific rules or principles.

In 5S terms, it means to distinguish between the necessary

and the unnecessary, to make the hard decisions, and to implement stratification management to get rid of the unnecessary.

The emphasis here is on stratification management and dealing with causes to get rid of the unnecessary and to nip causes before they become problems.

Stratification Management

In all kinds of situations and talking about all kinds of things, we speak of the need to be organized and refer casually to organizing and getting things in order. But, in fact, organization may well be the most important of the many things we do.

Just as there are some people who look completely helter-skelter but are actually very organized, so are there others who look neat and orderly but can never seem to find something when they want it. Organization is much more difficult than just putting things away. For example, anyone can clean up a messy room or desk, but only the owner can actually create a system and put things where they should be.

There are many different theories of how to organize your work, but the first step in all of these theories is to divide things and to group them in order of importance. The first thing is to create strata of importance and to implement stratification management. The Pareto diagram, the KJ method,* and even just taking inventory are all ways of organizing things, determining how important they are, and what the urgent imperatives are, and then preparing to do priority management. Whether it is to get rid of inventory that is not selling well or to make the seasonal switch, this is just another way of putting away or discarding the less-essential items so that you will be able to concentrate on the items that are really important and need your attention.

------

*The Pareto diagram and the KJ method (named after Vilfredo Pareto and Jiro Kawakita, respectively) are standard quality-control tools used in problem solving and in prioritizing and organizing information.

However, it is very difficult to distinguish between the essential and the non-essential at home and at work. At home, we have lots and lots of clothes that we never wear but just can't bring ourselves to get rid of. And at work, we have stacks of papers and bins of parts that we haven't needed since the second day we had them. But instead of practicing stratification management, we keep telling ourselves that someday we might have a use for this or that. We hang on to things just in case they might come in handy someday. But what we should be doing is making the hard decisions that we need to differentiate between the essential and the non-essential. We should be practicing stratification management.

Treating the Causes

That is why it is so important that we do a thorough house-cleaning and scrub away the accumulated trash. And when we do that, we will be able to see why things got this bad and we'll be able to get to the root of the problem. In effect, we'll be able to deal with the causes, and this is the important thing.

Seiton = Neatness

In general usage as in 5S usage, this means having things in the right places or right layout so they can be used in a hurry. It is a way of eliminating searches.

The emphasis here is on functional management and search elimination. Once everything has a right place so that it is functionally placed for quality and safety, you have a neat workplace.

Applying the Neatness Principle

The neatness principle applies throughout our society and to all aspects of our life. It is found in the card catalog system in the library, in the parking towers in our cities, in the system for reserving airline tickets, in layout analysis, in the way things are stored in the warehouse, in the way we arrange our dressers and cabinets at home, and even in the way we put things in our pockets. All of these arrangements require a certain amount of ingenuity. All of them are designed to enable us to find things when we want them and without a lot of needless searching and rummaging around. All are designed to give us ready access.

Functional Layout

Thus, it is that neatness starts with a detailed and intensive study of efficiency. Working from the organization stratification, the neatness principle seeks to formulate the rules governing this stratification. And more often than not, we start with a decision on how often we use things and work from there:

1. Things we don't use: discard.
2. Things we don't use but want to have on hand just in case: keep as contingency items.
3. Things we use only infrequently: store somewhere far away.
4. Things we use sometimes: store in the workplace.
5. Things we use frequently: keep at the workplace or on our persons.

Storage should also be based upon how much we have on hand and how soon we can get these things when we do need them. There is no need to keep a lot of something on hand when we can always get more in a hurry. Not only do we have to think about efficiency, we also need to talk about things such as quality, meaning rusting, marring, denting, deformation, and all the rest. Safety considerations also have to play a part in considering what the best, meaning the most functional, layout is. Are these things going to get dropped while they are being moved? Is the storage site safe? Have all the necessary precautions been taken in storing flammables? This is a very important and very difficult issue, demanding the utmost attention.

In order to keep the workplace looking orderly, it may well be necessary to draw passage lines and dividing lines on the floor. The layout has to be flexible so that it can be changed to satisfy new work requirements. Everything has to be up off the floor so that cleaning and inspections are both easy. The layout has to be such that it does not develop cobwebs, that the oil pans and other things can be accessed easily, and that the work goes smoothly.

Because neatness is to enhance efficiency, it is also important to do time studies, make improvements, and practice even during the straightening-up process. The ultimate aim of this straightening-up process is to be able to get as much as you want of something when and where you want it. And the key to doing this is to ask yourself the 5W's and the 1H (what, when, where, why, who, and how) for every item.

Seiso = **Cleaning**

In general usage, this means cleaning so that things are clean. In 5S terms, it means getting rid of waste, grime, and foreign matter and making things clean. Cleaning is a form of inspection.

The emphasis here is on cleaning as inspection, on cleanliness, and on creating an impeccable workplace.

Although cleaning obviously means eliminating waste and grime and making things clean, this has recently become increasingly important. With higher quality, higher precision, and finer processing technologies, even the smallest detail can have vital ramifications. That is why it is all the more important to be unyielding in your determination to do a thorough cleaning.

Inspection Sites

Some of your equipment and facilities will need to be kept especially spotless, and it is important that you know where

these places are. For example, those of you who are old enough
to remember the Tokyo Olympics will recall that the Japanese
women's volleyball team kept handkerchiefs tucked in at their
waists so they could wipe their brows from time to time, because they knew that sweat dripping on the court was a potential cause of slipping. And if they slipped, that could well cause
them to lose a point and hence the match. So for them, the
volleyball court was a priority inspection area.

The "To Clean Is To Inspect" Spirit

In the military, the rules are very strict about keeping guns
oiled and clean so they can be used at anytime. By extension,
modern factories have found that they will have fewer control
mistakes the more thorough they are about their cleaning procedures.

Cleaning does more than simply get the site and equipment
clean. It also provides an opportunity for inspection. Even the
places that are not dirty have to be checked and inspected.
Everything gets a good going-over when the cleaning is done
right, and that is why it has been said that to clean is to inspect.

This is true not just inside the factory. In fact, the factory
gate, the factory exterior, is the company's interface with the
community. Take a good look. Is the grass weed infested? Is
there litter strewn about? Imagine what kind of an impression
this makes. Does your factory look attractive, or does it look
like a slum? Even if you don't care about community relations,
how many good people are going to want to come to work for
a place that looks rundown? In this sense, the 5S's can be both
your ambassador to the community and your best recruiting
agent.

Achieving Zero Grime and Zero Dirt

Cleaning is thus something that can have a tremendous impact
on your downtime, quality, safety, morale, and every other
facet of the operation. It is the part that deserves your utmost
attention. That is why the 5S movement seeks to achieve zero

grime and zero dirt and to eliminate minor defects and minor faults at the key inspection points.

Seiketsu = Standardization

In 5S terms, standardization means continually and repeatedly maintaining your organization, neatness, and cleaning. As such, it embraces both personal cleanliness and the cleanliness of the environment.

The emphasis here is on visual management and 5S standardization. Innovation and total visual management are used to attain and maintain standardized conditions so that you can always act quickly.

Visual Management

Visual management has recently come into the limelight as an effective means of effecting *kaizen*. It is now being used for production, quality, safety, and everything else.

Color Management

Color management (or color-coding management) has also come in for considerable attention lately. This has been used not only for color-coding management, but also to create a work environment that is more conducive to work. There are more and more people in hands-on working positions that are opting for white and other light-colored clothes. And because these clothes show the dirt quickly, they provide a ready index of how clean things are. They highlight the need for ingenuity and action.

From the overall human perspective, hygiene has ramifications well beyond the factory, extending also to the environment. The 5S's are needed with regard to oil mist, filings, noise, thinner oils, toxic substances, and many more things found in the workplace to ensure that they do not foul up either the workplace or the broader environment. There are even companies that have taken to putting flowers in their workplaces, and this shows admirable spirit.

Shitsuke = Discipline

In general usage, this means training and the ability to do what you want to do even when it is difficult. In 5S terms, it means instilling (or having) the ability to do things the way they are supposed to be done.

The emphasis here is on creating a workplace with good habits and discipline. By teaching everyone what needs to be done and having everyone practice, bad habits are broken and good habits are formed. People get practice in making and following rules.

Discipline Is the First of the 5S's

Although there seems to be a bit of resistance to discipline among younger people because there is a feeling that it involves forcing people into preset behavioral patterns, it does not have to. People should not be that uptight about this. The word *shitsuke* originally comes from the first sewing that is done so that a kimono can be properly sewn. It is like the work that the tailor does before a fitting. In that sense, and once it is seen that way, it should be clear that discipline is something that we learn to make our lives go smoother. It is the basis of civilization. It is the minimum that we need for society to function. And that is why discipline should not be relegated to the end of the line in the 5S's or, much less, left out.

Discipline Can Change Behavioral Patterns

Discipline is a process of repetition and practice. Think, for example, of industrial safety. How many people have had accidents because they forgot to wear their hard hats, their safety shoes, or their goggles? Far too many. How many have had accidents because they stuck their hands into the machinery without shutting it off first? Again, too many. That is why it is so important that everyone be in the habit of obeying simple safety rules. That is why discipline is an integral part of industrial safety.

Whether it is emergency procedures, standard operating procedures, or whatever, it is crucial that every effort be made to get your people to do each and every step each and every time. There is no room for cutting corners or being embarrassed about looking like a beginner. Strict adherence is imperative. And to achieve this, you may need to take advantage of the morning meetings, you may want to have individual workers pledge their fidelity, you may want to institute one-point lessons, and you may want to do other things, but it is essential that everyone participate and participate fully.

An overview of the 5S words, their meaning, aims, activities, and principles, is found in Table 3.1. Typical 5S activities are found in Table 3.2.

3.2. PURPOSE OF THE 5S's

Because the 5S's seem so obviously important, many people make the mistake of concentrating on the individual terms as though these were some kind of good-luck charm. But it must be remembered that the 5S's are actually a means to achieving specific ends. And the 5S's have to be implemented with these objectives in mind.

Safety and the 5S's

For decades now, the two words *organization* and *neatness* have featured prominently on banners and newsletters even at small companies. Because safety is so important, and because organization and neatness are so important to safety, it is necessary to repeat these two terms time after time to make sure that the message is received by everyone.

TABLE 3.1. A 5S overview.

	Meaning	Aims	Activities	Principles
Organization (*Seiri*)	Distinguishing between the necessary and the unnecessary, and getting rid of what you do not need.	• Establish criteria and stick to them in eliminating the unnecessary. • Practice stratification management to set priorities. • Be able to deal with the causes of filth.	• Eliminating the unnecessary. • Dealing with the causes of filth. • *Kaizen* and standardization based on fundamentals.	Stratification management and dealing with the causes.
Neatness (*Seiton*)	Establishing a neat layout so you can always get just as much of what you need when you need it.	• A neat looking workplace. • Efficient (including quality and safety) layout and placement. • Raising productivity by eliminating the waste of looking for things.	• Functional storage based upon the 5W's and the 1H. • Practice and competition in putting things away and getting them out. • Neaten workplace and equipment. • Eliminating the waste of looking for things.	Functional storage and eliminating the need to look for things.

Cleaning (*Seiso*)	Eliminating trash, filth, and foreign matter for a cleaner workplace. Cleaning as a form of inspection.	• A degree of cleanliness commensurate to your needs. Achieving zero grime and zero dirt. • Finding minor problems with cleaning inspections. • Understanding that cleaning is inspecting.	• 5S's where it counts. • More efficient cleaning. • Cleaning and inspecting equipment and tools.	Cleaning as inspection and degrees of cleanliness.
Standardization (*Seiketsu*)	Keeping things organized, neat, and clean, even in personal and pollution-related aspects.	• Management standards for maintaining the 5S's. • Innovative visible management so that abnormalities show up.	• Innovative visible management. • Early detection and early action. • Tools (e.g., manuals) for maintaining standardization. • Color coding.	Visual management and 5S standardization.
Discipline (*Shitsuke*)	Doing the right thing as a matter of course.	• Full participation in developing good habits and workshops that follow the rules. • Communication and feedback as daily routine.	• One-minute 5S. • Communication and feedback. • Individual responsibility. • Practicing good habits.	Habit formation and a disciplined workplace.

TABLE 3.2. The 5S activities.

Theme	Typical Activities
Organization (*Seiri*): Stratification management and dealing with the causes.	1. Throw out the things you do not need. 2. Deal with the causes of dirt and leaks. 3. Housecleaning. 4. Treat defects and breakage. 5. Inspect covers and troughs to prevent leakage and scatter. 6. Clean the grounds. 7. Organize the warehouse. 8. Eliminate grime and burrs. 9. Eliminate oil pans.
Neatness (*Seiton*): Functional storage and eliminating the need to look for things.	1. Everything has a clearly designated place. 2. Thirty-second storage and retrieval. 3. Filing standards. 4. Zoning and placement marks. 5. Eliminate lids and locks. 6. First in, first out. 7. Neat notice boards. 8. Easy-to-read notices. 9. Straight lines and right angles. 10. Functional placement for materials, parts, carts, shelves, tools, equipment, and everything else.
Cleaning (*Seiso*): Cleaning as inspection and degrees of cleanliness.	1. Quick 5S drills. 2. Individual responsibility. 3. Make cleaning and inspection easier. 4. Sparkling clean campaigns. 5. Everybody is a janitor (priority 5S). 6. Perform cleaning inspections and correct minor problems. 7. Clean even the places most people do not notice.

Standardization (*Seiketsu*):
Visual management and 5S standardization.

1. Okay marks.
2. Danger zones marked on meters.
3. Thermal labels.
4. Directional markings.
5. Belt-size labels.
6. Open-and-shut directional labels.
7. Voltage labels.
8. Color-coded pipes.
9. Oil labels.
10. Warning colors.
11. Fire extinguisher signs.
12. Foolproofing.
13. Responsibility labels.
14. Wire management.
15. Inspection marks.
16. Precision-maintenance labels.
17. Limit labels.
18. Color coding.
19. Transparency.
20. Preventing noise and vibration.
21. "I-can-do-it-blindfolded" placement.
22. 5S calendars.
23. Parklike plant setting.

Discipline (*Shitsuke*):
Habit formation and a disciplined workplace.

1. All-together cleaning.
2. Exercise time.
3. Pick-up practice.
4. Wear your safety shoes.
5. Public-space management.
6. Practice dealing with emergencies.
7. Individual responsibility.
8. Telephone and communication practice.
9. 5S manuals.
10. Seeing is believing.

Emphasizing the orderly workplace. But what this really means is that you have to pay attention to the little things. Are you wearing your hard hat and safety shoes? Are you being careful when you transport things? Are the paths clear? It is these little things—these seemingly insignificant things—that make the difference. That is why people have emphasized the importance of an orderly workplace. In addition to these things, the 5S's are also important to personal safety and health for everyone in preventing fires and slippage accidents due to oil leaks, in preventing pollution from filings and fumes, and in preventing the other things that are so dangerous to human health and safety.

The workplace that is conscientious about the 5S's does not have to keep harping on safety, and it has fewer industrial accidents than the factory that only emphasizes foolproofing equipment and procedures.

Efficiency and the 5S's

The craftsman takes care of his tools. The famous chef, the skilled carpenter, the great painter—they all take care of their tools. There are no rusted knives, no saws with teeth missing, and no matted brushes. They use good tools, and they take good care of them. They do not waste a lot of time when they are working. They know that the time spent taking care of their tools is not time wasted—that that save far more time because their tools are in good condition than they spend making sure that they are that way.

Even 3 minutes can make a difference. Organization and neatness might not make much of a difference when you have all the time in the world, but it does count when you are working to a tight schedule. That is why it is useful to think of the 5S's as part of this schedule. Do not spend too much time on the 5S activities. Set aside a short period of time when everyone will concentrate on the 5S's. One day it might be to make sure everything is in place. Another day it might be to make sure there are no oil leaks. It can be anything, but it is important that everybody be involved in this for a short time.

For example, some companies have instituted 3-minute 5S periods. Everybody knows what they are supposed to do, and they know that they only have 3 minutes to do it. And they are all working on the 5S's at the same time. You will be surprised at how much can be accomplished if your people have had practice in the 5S's and they know what they are supposed to do. This is also a useful way to mark the beginning or end of the work day. It is only 3 minutes, but it means vastly better efficiency in the long run.

Quality and the 5S's

Modern electronics and other machinery demand very high levels of precision and cleanliness. Just a spot of grime can cause a computer to crash. Filings and burrs can mean that things do not fit tightly. Dropping things on an assembly line can mean that the wrong parts are put together or that the product is shipped to the wrong client. There are all kinds of major problems caused by seemingly minor 5S lapses. It is clear that the 5S's are prerequisite to quality, and this cannot be overemphasized.

Breakdowns and the 5S's

There is a common "Monday Morning Syndrome" at some manufacturing plants. This is where sludge-clogged oil drains overflow on Monday morning, where the machinery seems to stick on Monday morning, and where hydraulic and pneumatic equipment pressure levels are low on Monday morning. All of these things happen because the buildup of grime over the course of the work week has had time to harden and to settle into places where it should not be. All of these things happen because the company does not practice the 5S's during the week.

People have the same problem. When they are doing something every day, they get into a routine. Yet when they come back after a vacation, they forget which way this valve should be turned, which way is off for this switch, and what readings are normal for this meter. All of these things should be marked. But all too often, they are not. All too often, the company (and the worker) assumes that no labels are needed. And then when they come back from vacation, they find out how faulty memory can be.

Practicing the 5S's—making sure that you have a neat workplace, that things are not in the way but where you can get them when you need them, and creating "a good place to work" will save money in the long run. It will improve quality, raise efficiency, enhance safety, and cure the Monday Morning Syndrome of defective products and injured workers.

SUMMARY

- The 5S activities are actions that people take and things that people do. And the results are in direct proportion to the effort made. Yet it is difficult to quantify the 5S's, and this emphasis on empirical proof makes some people skeptical. Nevertheless, the 5S's are basic to everything you do, and results are bound to show up. Company after company has had the same experience. So resolve to do your best, and soon you will be the best.

- Each of the 5S words is simple enough in itself, yet each has a depth of meaning and significance for the workplace. However, because they have entered common usage, people tend to think they are not sophisticated and hence not "modern." People tend to understand them as meaning many different things. It is essential that you make sure everybody has the same understanding of the terms and their meaning—that everyone is doing the same thing. Sometimes this will mean developing special action programs for specific purposes.

- It is easy to start the 5S activities, but it is very difficult to maintain a steady pace and to become truly proficient in all of their aspects. But if you do not keep moving forward, you will find yourself backsliding. What should each person be doing? How? Why? It is essential that everyone be committed to implementing the 5S's all the time.

Chapter 4

Seiri = *Organization*

4.1. ORGANIZATION TECHNOLOGY

People have talked about the importance of organization for centuries. Generation after generation has been reminded of the need to not just rush in and out of things, but to attend to organization. And history teaches that people who ignore organization all too often tend to lose sight of their objectives and even of their means. In trying to build a levy to reclaim new orchard land, for example, it is important to chart the flow of water, to design a levy that will channel that flow easily and without breaking, and to build the levy carefully so that it holds under pressure. All of this takes organization.

Even so, there seems to have been a spate of magazine articles and books about organization. What is significant about this outpouring is that it marks organization's transition from a common-sensical concept that people could be relied upon to apply on their own to an academic discipline demanding study and thought.

Deciding on Means and Ends

When the land was poor and there was not enough of anything to go around, it was enough to be as frugal and savings-minded as possible. It was a good idea to save everything, somewhat like a pack rat. This was a time when people would hold on to the least little thing because it seemed such a waste to throw anything away. Yet today, when we seem to be overwhelmed with an abundance of goods, services, and information, it is more important to be able to sort through these things than it is to save each and every little piece. By looking at information alone, there is a whole new career field called *information management* that does nothing but sort through information and organize it. It is important to save things, but it is just as important to throw things out. And most important of all is knowing what to discard, what to save, and how to save things so that they can be accessed later.

In doing this organization, the first thing is to define the objectives. Why are you doing this? Once you know that, you are in a position to decide how to go about it. There are all kinds of methods available—the KJ method, Pareto analysis, taking inventory, functional analysis, and the kind of numbering that the library does for its card catalog. The trick is to decide what you will want these things for later and then how you can get rid of the ones you do not need and still keep the rest of them easily accessible but not in the way.

The Art of Throwing Things Away

Kyoto University Professor Yuji Aida does his organization with what he calls the Aida Method. His feeling is that saving things and information indiscriminately just takes extra space and creates more work—that it is important to get rid of the things you don't need.

When he gets to the university each day, he takes the mail out of his box in the department office and glances through it on the stairs and in the hall on the way to his office. As he is walking, he separates the things he wants to keep from the things he does not want to keep. And then the things that failed to pass this initial screening get dumped in the wastebasket just inside his door. Doing this, he often finds that he has nothing left by the time he sits down at his desk.

Organization is truly the art of throwing things away (see Figure 4.1).

4.2. THE CRUX OF ORGANIZATION

One of the key points in organization is that of defining what constitutes organization. How do you know if you are organ-

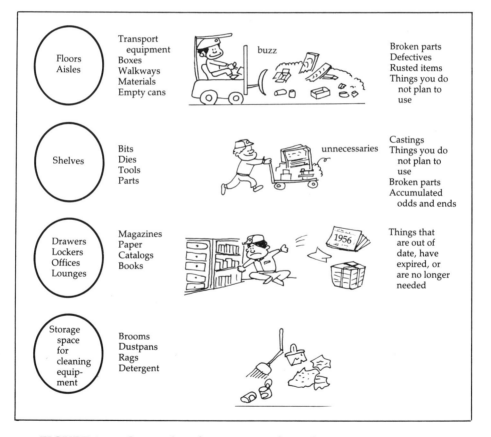

FIGURE 4.1.   Separating the necessary from the unnecessary.

ized or not? What are the principles that come into play here? When you decide to implement organization, how do you know when to stop?

Although it was stated before that organization is the art of throwing things away, this should perhaps be amended, because throwing things away is only the first step—even if it is the crucial first step. Start by getting rid of everything you do not need. And while you are at it, it would be a good idea to pay special attention to equipment that does not work right and to broken parts (see Figure 4.2).

Clearly, this idea of throwing out everything you do not need has to entail value judgments and stratification management. And if you do it right, it will also entail cleaning oil-soiled places and places where grime has piled up so badly that you cannot see if they are in savable shape or not. You will not know if you need something—that is, how useful it is—until you see it looking its best and most functional.

Stratification by importance and deciding where to store things.   Stratification management involves deciding how important something is and then moving both to cut down on non-essential inventory and at the same time ensuring that the things that are essential are close at hand for maximum efficiency. Thus the key to good stratification management is the ability to make these decisions about usage frequency (which is just another way of saying importance) and to ensure that things are in their proper places (see Table 4.1). It is just as important to have the things you do not need far from hand as it is to have the things you do need close at hand (see Table 4.2). It is just as important to be able to throw out a broken or defective part as it is to be able to fix it.

Once stratification and classification are done, you are in a position to decide what you want to do with things that you do not use more than once a year, if that. Save them or throw them away? And if you decide to save them, how much of them do you need to save? It is safe to assume you need less of something the less frequently you use it. And when you do this kind of major housecleaning, it is not at all uncommon for

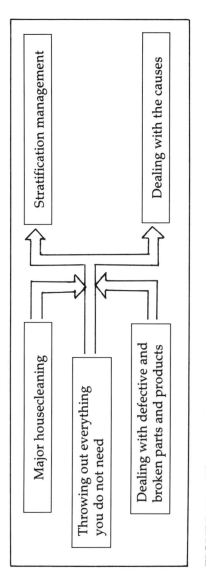

FIGURE 4.2. The organization process.

TABLE 4.1. The crux of organization.

	Degree of Need (Frequency of Use)	Storage Method (Stratification)
Low	• Things you have not used in the past year • Things you have only used once in the last 6–12 months	• Throw them out • Store at a distance
Average	• Things you have only used once in the last 2–6 months • Things used more than once a month	• Store in central place in the workplace
High	• Things used once a week • Things used every day • Things used hourly	• Store near the work site or carry on the person

you to find you have tons of junk on hand—tons of stuff you do not need. Do the housecleaning again, and you'll find you still have tons of things you don't need. This is a never-ending process.

TABLE 4.2. Storing the things you need.

Item	Storage
Things you use especially often	Keep them within easy reach
Things in constant use	Keep them easy to get out, easy to put away, and easy to understand where they should be
Things you use sometimes	Be sure to put them back where they belong, which means a board with pictures, color coding, and more
Files	Number and color code them for both shelf and order

This is true not only because things tend to collect, but also because it is very difficult to distinguish between what you need and what you don't need, and because most people tend to err in the beginning on the conservative side of saving things "just in case." But it is crucial that management make a decision. Is it needed? If not, get rid of it. If yes, how much is needed? Get rid of the rest.

4.3. GETTING RID OF THE UNNECESSARY

Approaching the Task

In starting to get rid of the unnecessary, your approach will vary somewhat, depending on whether you decided to worry just about getting rid of things you don't need, to also deal with broken machinery and tools at the same time, or even to combine this with a major housecleaning. You will have to decide each time how extensive—how big a project—you want this to be. However, most people opt to do a thorough job and to couple this with a major housecleaning.

Going About the Task

In going about the task of getting rid of the unnecessary, the usual progression is as follows:

1. Decide on the scope of the operation (what workplaces and zones) and the targets that you want to achieve.
2. Get ready.
3. Teach people to recognize what is unnecessary.
4. Quantify and assess.
5. Perform management inspection and assessment, and provide pointers on how to do better next time.

Decide on the Scope of the Operation and the Targets

Because it is sometimes very difficult to decide what you need and what you do not need, it is often helpful to decide ahead of time how much trash you are going to throw out. For example, you might decide that you are going to pare your stock of bits by half. Or you might decide that you are just going to save one box of each thing. Or you might say that you plan to fill so many two-ton trucks.

At the same time, it is also important to delineate exactly what workplaces or zones you are going to go through. You might decide to do a different section each month. Be careful, however, that you do not leave out any sections.

Get Ready

This is primarily a process of going through the 5W's and the 1H. Who is going to do what? Where? When? How? And, of course, why? It is especially important to cover all the details here, including how the trash is going to be moved out and all of the safety concerns.

Teach People to Recognize What is Unnecessary

Unless this is done with great care and thoroughness, it will be necessary to do the organization again and again—each time adding more instruction. There are a number of points that have to be covered, as explained in the next section, but it is crucial that everyone know exactly what is supposed to be done and how.

Quantify and Assess

Be sure to keep a record of everything that is carted out—what it is and how much of it. Make the decisions and assessments. Is it to be discarded? Is it to be stored in a somewhat distant warehouse? Is it needed somewhere else? Should it be fixed? These and other questions will occur for every item that is removed, and somebody has to make the decisions. There is no point in carting things out if you are just going to cart them back in again.

It is crucial here that you not let yourself fall prey to doubt. Do not think it is "such a waste to throw it out." Remember the efficiency you are buying. Do not even consider saving it just temporarily or "for the time being until a decision can be made." Forget that you might—just might—want that some day. If something is borrowed, return it to its owner. Don't worry about not having a lot of "maybe" items on hand. Be firm with yourself, and stick to your resolve.

Perform Management Inspection and Assessment, and Provide Pointers

In this stage, management should visit the shop, inspect the progress that has been made, and give advice on what else might be done. It is most important to be thorough about this. In some companies, management has even had people take everything off the shelves and out of the lockers and then justify anything they wanted to put back. What cannot be justified should not be there in the first place.

4.4. IDENTIFYING UNNECESSARIES

There are a number of places where things nobody is using and nobody needs seem to collect.

Shelves and Lockers

Somehow, the backs of shelves and lockers seem to collect things that nobody ever uses, the surplus—and the broken.

You will also find a lot of things you do not need on the top or bottom shelves (see Photo 4.1).

Sometimes you may even find boxes of personal belongings.

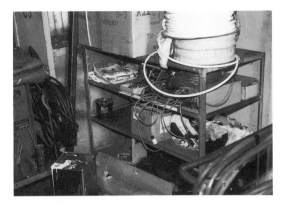

PHOTO 4.1.   Shelves of junk.

Passageways and Corners

Like dust, things you do not need seem to gather in the corners.

Beside the passageways, between the passageways and the walls, and especially the little-used passageways are also convenient places for people to put things and forget them.

Parts and Work in Progress

You will find things that have fallen back behind the machinery or rolled under it. Sometimes there will even be broken items inside the machinery.

There will be things under the carts.

Very often you will find that you have extra work in progress. You may also find that you have considerable stocks of defectives.

There will be small stocks left of parts and materials that are no longer in use. There will be old parts and materials lying about when you do not use FIFO (first in, first out) inventory control.

Bits, Tools, Jigs, and Measurement Devices

Very often you will find that you have larger stocks than you need of these things—or that you even have the broken ones still lying about because no one thought to throw them out.

There are things that you don't need right away—things you never will need again. Throw them out.

Contingency Parts

More often than not, the storage space for contingency parts has become a last refuge for broken parts, surplus, and things that nobody is ever going to need. When people root through the bins for something, they take out the good ones and leave the bad ones in. And over the years you develop whole bins of bad parts.

Beside Pillars and Under the Stairs

Because these are shadowy places, they tend to collect junk and not get cleaned out. Clean them out.

Machinery, Stands, Racks, and Carts

You will find that you have extra machinery, bearing heads, stands, racks, and all the rest.

There will be extra extension cords, tubing, piping, lighting equipment, switches, and all of the other things that you thought you might need someday but haven't needed for the last five years and couldn't find even if you did need them. Get rid of them.

Floors, Pits, and Partitions

Things fall or are placed on the floor for all kinds of reasons, and then they stay there (see Photo 4.2). There are materials,

PHOTO 4.2.   Junk on the floor.

work in progress, defective parts, fixtures, and almost everything else down there.

Even tools are dropped and never picked up.

Storehouses and Sheds

Out of sight and out of mind, these places tend to become
regular junk heaps (see Photo 4.3).

**PHOTO 4.3.   Storage sheds need to be
cleaned out.**

Walls and Bulletin Boards

There are notices that have long since lost any relevance they might have had. There are notes and schedules that have turned yellow with age. There are scraps of paper that do not mean anything any more. There are all kinds of things posted on walls and bulletin boards. This is just as unsightly and wasteful as the junk that piles up alongside the wall (see Photo 4.4).

Outside

Look near the fence. Look around the outside of buildings. Look at the drainage pipes. Look at the eaves and along the paths. How much junk is there? And you can be sure that anything out here is not going to be needed tomorrow.

In all of this, be especially thorough and rigorous about any place that has a lid or a lock on it.

PHOTO 4.4. Junk along the wall.

4.5. UNDERTAKING A MAJOR HOUSECLEANING

How To Do a Major Housecleaning

Major housecleanings can be done in conjunction with campaigns to deal with the causes of grime and soiling, but they are better done independently.

How you do the major housecleaning will very much depend on what it is you are cleaning up. For example:

- Oil and other liquids will have to be removed with pumps.
- Soot, filings, and the like will have to be removed with a broom and a shovel.
- Dirty surfaces, crud-encrusted places, and oil-stained panels will have to be cleaned with wire brushes and polishing equipment. Very often, you may have to use high-pressure cleaning techniques, and the dirty windows and floors will probably have to be done several times.
- Rust and corrosion will have to be removed carefully to avoid breaking weak parts.
- And seasonal considerations are important in policing the grounds.

Points to Remember

Your major housecleaning has to go from the rooftops to the underslung pits. It has to deal with each piece of equipment separately. And it may have to include the outside grounds as well (see Photo 4.5). Yet extensive though the work will be and busy though everyone will be, there are several points that absolutely have to be borne in mind for safety and breakage-prevention considerations.

Safety

Just as people can slip and fall from high places, things can fall on people working on the floors or in the pits.

Be absolutely sure all of the equipment and power is off

Before

After

PHOTO 4.5. Before and after a 5S house-cleaning.

when you have people climbing on the machinery or crawling under it.

Detergents are slippery and chemical cleaners may be toxic. Be careful.

People will be working with blasters and other unfamiliar equipment. Make sure they know what they are doing and how to use the equipment safely.

Breakage Prevention

It sometimes happens that the machinery doesn't work after a major housecleaning. Detergent may have gotten in some-where and blocked a passage. Water may have gotten in and the machinery may have started to rust. Something may have been accidentally moved a little out of alignment. There are all kinds of possible causes.

Also, people working in the pits, cleaning high places, and doing other jobs may get drenched from head to foot. They may find that they are black with soot when they get done. So it is important to wear old clothes. Some people may even want to wear protective gear.

The longer this housecleaning is put off, the longer it is likely to take. If there are heavily encrusted places, a hammer and chisel may have to be used to even start to get them clean (see Photo 4.6).

Before

After

PHOTO 4.6. Before and after cleaning.

4.6. GETTING RID OF THINGS THAT ARE BROKEN

Although this is basically the same as the major push to get rid of things you do not need, there may be some things that you do not need or cannot use but cannot just take and throw out. That is why it is important to make a thorough inspection of all the places where you have problems. It might even be a good idea to get out a floor plan of the plant and go around marking a big P anywhere there is a problem. If there are a lot of P's, the work will be long and difficult.

Everything should be covered: buildings, roofs, windows, pillars, electrical cords, light bulbs, switches, stands, shelves, lockers, machinery, plaques, storage bins, and all the rest. Look for breakage, rust, misalignment, careless placement, scratching, grime, and everything else that might be wrong. Anything you can see that's wrong needs to be fixed. List everything. Some things you'll be able to fix quickly and easily. Other things will be more difficult. Decide which is which. Some things you'll be able to fix with in-house people, and others will require outside expertise. Again, decide which is which. A sample checklist is found in Table 4.3.

4.7. DEALING WITH THE CAUSES

Why Deal With the Causes?

People are the main cause of contamination in the electronics industry and in medical care facilities. That is why there are air locks, air showers, special clothing, and all the rest. It used to be that the electronics industry spent a lot of time and energy on such things as cleaning, deburring, polishing, and sealing, but now it spends even more time and energy on building and maintaining clean rooms.

One recent trend in industry is for all kinds of companies—not just electronics and medical equipment but even machine tools and all kinds of manufacturers—to be very concerned

TABLE 4.3. Sample checklist.

Category	Items to be Checked	Score	Comments
1. Safety equipment	1. Is safety equipment worn properly? 2. Does the safety equipment work properly? 3. Are the warnings adequate? 4. Are all the ''fire prohibited,'' ''volatile solvent,'' ''high-pressure equipment,'' and other signs there? 5. Are gas tanks braced so they will not fall over?		
2. Protective covers	1. Do all the places that need protective covers have them? 2. Are they all in place, with no breakage or misalignment? 3. Is it easy to see in and under them?		
3. Fire-fighting equipment	1. Are the fire extinguishers clean and in place (right number, right places)? 2. Are the fire hoses and warning equipment clearly marked? 3. Are the hoses in good shape? 4. Are the hoses put away correctly?		
4. Others	1. Is the work environment good (includes vibration, noise, soot, gases, heat, wind, etc.)?		

with precision and to recognize that environmental control is an important part of ensuring product precision.

At one plant, spotting even a single drop of leaked oil sets off the workers and they track the leak back to its origins. And because the workers are so intent on stopping oil leaks, they have not had very many to stop for quite some time.

There are a number of reasons why it is difficult to implement and enforce a policy of tracking things down to their causes. Some of the most common are as follows:

1. People accept the status quo as a given. They do not realize how good things could be, and they assume that things have always been—and always will be—the way they are.
2. There are too many other problems. There are broken machinery and worn-out tools, and it gets so things are so dilapidated that it is impossible to trace a problem back to its origins.
3. People have given up. All too often, they have found that it is difficult to maintain cleanliness and they have resigned themselves to filth and all of the problems that go with it.
4. Technology is lacking. Very often people do not know enough to think of the technological fix that is needed—or to implement it even if they do think of it.

Procedures For Tracking Grime To Its Origins

The seven simple steps for tracking grime to its origins are shown in Figure 4.3.

Defining Grime and Its Location and Form

The first imperative is that of clearly identifying the grime. Even before you start trying to track the grime back to its origins, it is important to identify clearly what grime is. This means identifying the kinds and locations of grime, how far

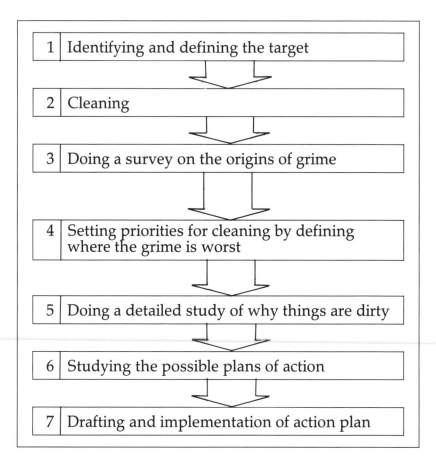

FIGURE 4.3.   Tracking grime to its origins.

back it is, and how much there is, because this problem defini-
tion will determine how you go about your cleaning and how
you structure your problem solving. Very broadly, grime may
be classified as shown in Table 4.4.

It is important to note here that you cannot track grime
back to its origins if everything is filthy. This can only be done
during or right after a major housecleaning.

TABLE 4.4. Types of leakage and grime.

How Carried or Spread	Type								Explanation
	Oil	Steam and Water	Air and Gas	Burrs and Filings	Sand and Dust	Pellets	Oil Mist	Parts and Materials	
Airborne	○	○		○	○	○	○	○	Escapes from holes or cracks
Overflow	○	○	○	○	○	○		○	Overflow from full containers
Sticking	○	○		○	○	○		○	Sticks to people, equipment, carts, and materials
Spillage	○	○		○	○	○		○	Spilled while replenishing, collecting, disposing, cleaning, or the like
Spreads	○	○					○		Liquids spread along wires, pipes, etc., and leak
Seepage	○	○	○				○		Seeps out from holes or cracks
Falls	○	○						○	Things fall from shelves, conveyor belts, or the like

Surveying For the Causes of Grime

Cleanliness policy means making sure that everything is clean, but it is a little more complicated than just starting a drive to have everyone participate in clean-up campaigns. Indeed, the saddest sight is a workplace where they just clean up where things are dirty and then consider the job done. Cleaning up is important, but that is just the start. It is important to do a causal survey and keep the place clean.

Tracking Down Grime Scientifically

What is grime? Why is it a problem? What are the tolerable limits? These and other questions have to be considered and answered if the causal survey is to mean anything. Is this particular grime caused by a leak somewhere, or was it tracked in, or were there impurities, or was it blown in, or did something fall, etc.? There are many different possible causes, and that it why it is so important to look at the grime and categorize it.

Is this grime something that is a normal occurrence in the production process, or is it something that you would not expect to have happen? Is it something that should be prevented? Was it just because someone was careless? Or is there maybe so much grime that people just do not have time to get around to it all? You need to approach this scientifically. How did the grime get there, and how can it be prevented? Otherwise your efforts will not have any real impact.

Ranking Filthiness

Specifically, it might be important to attach tags to the different places that are grimy. They could state exactly where the grime is, what conditions are like, how much grime there is, and other factors. This assessment is very important (see Table 4.5). In addition, they could tell what is being done at present to prevent grime buildups and what cleaning methods are being used.

Once this survey is done, you are ready to rank the Worst Ten or whatever. You are ready to set priorities. Of course, covers that do not fit right or shielding that is bent should be fixed immediately, but it is still important to set priorities on the more difficult problems.

Next, start with your priority locations and try to determine why they are so dirty.

- Is dust collection and ventilation what it should be?
- Is this a place where filings and dust tend to collect?
- Are the packings and sealings tight in places where a lot of dust is generated?
- Are the equipment, cover, sheeting, and other things in good shape?
- What can be done to prevent oil and water from splashing?

There is much more to add to this, so much that the list is almost endless. For example, you might also want to look at whether these are problems that the workplace can solve on its own or whether you need to call for technical assistance. In this grime-prevention campaign (which is to say this 5S campaign), it is important that you quantify things such as where the grime is, what kind of grime it is, how much of it there is, and how it can be prevented—and that you look at how the problem might or might not relate to the specific equipment, tools, or processes being used at that particular workplace.

Drawing Up An Action Plan

There are two main ways to draw up an action plan.

Dealing With Causes

The first way is to see to it that the grime does not happen. Whether this is taken to mean eliminating all grime at the

TABLE 4.5.   Mapping out a plan of action against sand leakage.

	Line: CSS-6		Sand Leakage Map							
	Location		Assessment							
			Kind of Leakage					Amt.	Cond.	Recovery
Map No.	Equipt.	Part	Air-borne	Over-flow	Along wires, etc.		On cases	Shovels per day	Condition of covers, etc.	Time per day or week
1	BC103	head		O				5		0.1h/d
2	BC104	···		O				7	···	0.25h/d
3	BC105	head						2		0.25h/d
4	FS-5	valve	O					2/day	none	
5		plate cleaner	O					2/day	none	
6	F-10	···unit						5/day	none	10h/wk
7	PE-40	overhead PS					O	3/day	none	
8	MO-90	form		O	O					
9	BC139	···		O				10/day	···	0.25h/d
10	BC139	BC140 ···		O	O			20/day	···	0.5h/d
11	BC139	BC138 ···		O	O			30/day	···	1.0h/d

source or only holding it down to manageable levels, it still involves an effort to come to grips with grime at the source. This requires utilizing all of the technological tools at your command. It may also mean a major effort to fix everything that is broken and to ensure that things stay fixed day in and day out.

Dealing With the Hard-To-Clean Places

The second approach is to assume that the work inevitably entails some grime and to make an effort to develop more

Div.	Sec.	Dept.		Date:	November 25	Section No.	
				Inspector: Sunaga		Line No.	1/2

Steps to be Taken

Recovery Efficiency				Method			Section			Cost	Schedule		Results
Y	N	Equipment (scraper, vacuum cleaner, etc.)	Prior-ity	Fix	Im-prove	Re-place	In-shop	Re-pair shop	Ma-chine shop		In	Out	× Assess-ment
	O	brooms & shovels	27										
	O	shovels	16										
	O		17		O								
	O		28		O								
	O		22		O				O				
	O		23		O				O				
	O		29		O				O				
	O	...	30		O				O				
O		widen head	8	O	O			O	O				
O		...	4		O								
O			1										

efficient ways of cleaning. Of the two, this is the more familiar approach. For example, it might mean redesigning the oil and water runoff gutters so that all the waste comes to one place for treatment and disposal rather than going every which way. It might mean redesigning equipment so that it is easier to clean. It might mean designing things so that shavings fall off the machinery rather than pile up. In effect, it means eliminating hard-to-clean places. (See Figure 4.4.)

Once you have drawn up an action plan, it is important to review it once more to see how much it will cost to implement,

Approach	Specific Techniques (5S Techniques)		Measures
1. Preventing grime i. Prevention ii. Reduction	Preventing leakage:	Enclosing, sealing	1. Remove
	Preventing splashing:	Doors, cover design, directing flow	2. Wipe
			3. Fix
	Preventing falling:	Transport means, insertion means, case design	4. Cease
			5. Stop
Dealing with the causes	Fixing loosening and breakage		6. Reduce
	Process research:	Burr-free, oilless, no-polish	7. Don't save up
	Clogging, clog prevention		8. Collect
			9. Don't spill
2. Collection & removal i. Collection ii. Removal	Review dust-collection methods		
		Capacity, duct inlet sizes, etc.	10. Don't walk around with
	Review collection and removal methods		
		Cleaning tools, drainage gutters, container shapes, container sizes, etc.	11. Chip off
Dealing with hard-to-clean places	Review cleaning methods		
	Shape of filings:	Size, direction of flight, etc.	
	Equipment itself, base shape, etc.		

FIGURE 4.4.   Dealing with grime.

what new equipment might be needed, and even whether or not you will be able to do it with in-house people or will have to call in outside help. In this process, it is also important to define how much of an impact the plan can be expected to have and to set priorities.

Tenacity is the most important quality in dealing with the causes of grime.

But how are you going to survey how grime arises? And just because you have drawn up one action plan is no reason to stop. Only after the plan has been revised and refined again and again will it start to have an impact. Even though much more work is needed on grime-prevention techniques, most companies do not put enough effort into this.

The technical problems are different if this is grime or a leak, but either way it is crucial that the company develop the technological capability to deal with this.

FLESHING OUT THE ACTION PLAN

Getting rid of oil pans and redesigning covers and sheeting.   Oil leakage is a major problem at most manufacturing facilities. As a result, most factories have oil pans to catch the leaking oil. However, this simply disguises the problem, and it is better to get rid of the oil pans and to strive for a panless factory. Getting rid of oil pans will force you to examine where the leakage is coming from, what is causing it, and how to fix it. Where the leaks cannot be stopped, you might want to install drainage pipes rather than just have the oil sit in a pan collecting dust.

Smaller covers.   Rather than trying to cover the whole piece of equipment where there is oil leakage or filings, it is better to move closer to the actual sources and to design smaller covers or sheeting for just those locations (see Photo 4.7).

Others.   Other policies that might be considered include robot aprons, movable covers, and more. The important thing is that you innovate and that everybody at the workplace be oriented toward identifying the specific causes.

SUMMARY

- Organization means having things in their right places. It means solving problems at their origins. This is the highest priority among the 5S. Start with organization at the workplace. Do you have piles of things you do not need? Get rid of them. This is fundamental to everyday management.

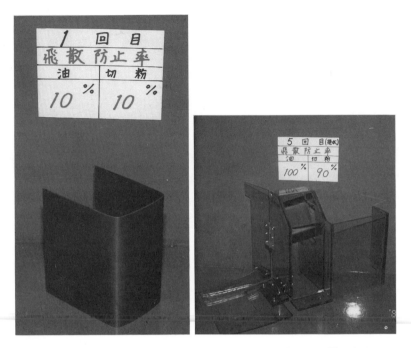

PHOTO 4.7. Custom-made covers. Signs indicate effectiveness ratings for two covers (original model—left; later model—right) designed to contain oil and filings.

- This has to be initiated from above, because the individual worker is usually so wrapped up in the work or so used to the way things are done that he or she does not notice the need for organization. There must be repeated efforts to get rid of things you do not need, because it is very difficult to throw everything out all at once. It has been said that the people who are best at moving are those who do not have a lot of things to move. That is why it is so important to stratify and to be clear on the criteria for stratification.

- The same is true of dealing with the causes of soiling. Cleaning has to be done every day, but even then you will never be able to keep up unless you eliminate some of the need for cleaning. You have to study why things are so dirty and what can be done to prevent this. This is the sort of thing the people at the workplace should be good at.

- Except for major technological problems, you will probably not have to involve outside help in solving these problems. For the most part, it is a constant campaign to have the people at the workplace make the improvements, look at the results, and then make more improvements.

Chapter 5

Seiton = *Neatness*

5.1. NEATNESS TECHNOLOGY

Putting things away the way you should. After you have gotten rid of all the things you do not need, the next question is to make the decisions on how many of what should be put where. This is neatness. As such, *neatness* means putting things away with efficiency, quality, and safety in mind, and it means questing for the optimum way to put things away.

There are innumerable examples of organization and neatness in everyday life. Parking lots are one. All of the cars are parked efficiently so that any one of them can be moved when needed. The way books are arranged in the library is another. So is systematic layout planning, warehouse management, the layout of tools in the workplace, and even the way things are arranged on the grocery store shelf. It is not a difficult concept to visualize and appreciate. It is just difficult to do.

Yet it is not even difficult if three simple rules are followed.

73

Decide Where Things Belong

The first step is to decide where things belong. Of course, there need to be criteria for deciding this, because the absence of criteria and any pattern will make it impossible for people to remember where things are supposed to be and will mean that it takes that much longer for them to put things back or to get them out. Yet there are many possibilities, and selecting the one that is best for you will take some study.

Decide How Things Should Be Put Away

Next is to decide how things should be put away. This is critical to functional storage. Things should be put away so they are easy to find and easy to access. Storage has to be done with retrieval in mind.

Obey the Put-Away Rules

The third rule is to obey the rules. This means always putting things back where they belong. It sounds simple, and it is if you do it. It is just doing it that is difficult. Whether or not this is done will determine whether or not organization and neatness succeeds. At the same time, inventory management is important to see that you do not run out of parts or products.

5.2. PROMOTING NEATNESS

The basic procedure for neatness is (1) analyze the status quo, (2) decide where things belong, (3) decide how things should be put away, and (4) get everybody to follow the put-away rules (see Figure 5.1).

5.3. UNDERSTANDING AND ANALYZING THE STATUS QUO

Neatness is a study in efficiency. It is a question of how quickly you can get the things you need and how quickly you can put

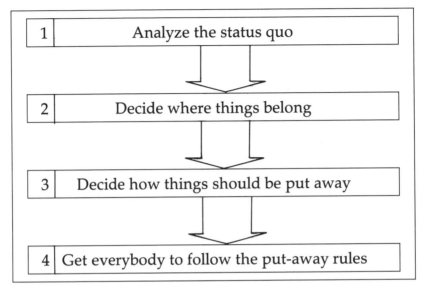

FIGURE 5.1. **Promoting neatness.**

them away. Just making an arbitrary decision on where things go is not going to make you any faster. Instead, you have to analyze why getting things out and putting them away takes so long. You have to study this for both the new workers and the shop veterans.

You have to devise a system that everyone can understand. Otherwise, all your efforts will be for naught.

Start with analysis. Start by analyzing how people get things out and put them away, and why it takes so long. This is especially important in workplaces that use a lot of different tools and materials, because time spent getting things out and putting them away is time lost. For example, if a person gets something out or puts something away 200 times a day and each time takes 30 seconds, you are talking about 100 minutes—more than an hour and a half—a day. If the average time could be reduced to 10 seconds, you could save more than an hour. (See Photo 5.1.)

When you are dealing with small-lot production and quick

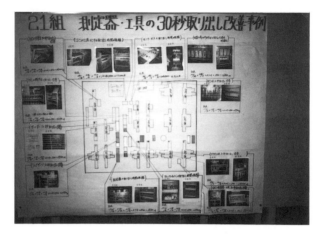

PHOTO 5.1. Poster explaining 30-second put-away.

turnaround times, every second counts. A minute spent getting something out and putting it away could be fatal. One manufacturer who did a detailed study of the logistics of the materials and tools used in the production process found that,

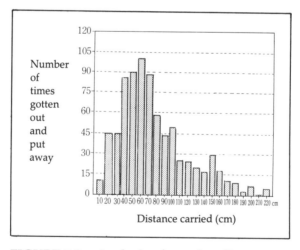

FIGURE 5.2. Analysis of carrying distances.

difficulty levels aside, there was considerable variation in how far things had to be carried. (See Figure 5.2.)

At this shop, the total carriage distance for an average day was 180 kilometers. They also found that making all of the distances between 40 and 60 centimeters would yield considerably better efficiency. Thus, they instituted organization and neatness to standardize the work flow and improve the work process. (See Table 5.1.)

TABLE 5.1.   Sample analysis of retrieval times.

No.	Work	Time	Problems
1	Ask name		1. Do not know what things are called 2. Find out
2	Retrieval		1. Not sure where things are kept 2. Storage site far away 3. Storage sites scattered all around 4. Repeat trips
3	Search		1. Hard to find because many things are there 2. Not labeled 3. Not there, but not clear whether it is out or somebody is using it 4. Unclear if spares exist (no ledger and nowhere to ask) 5. One brought was defective
4	Retrieve		1. Hard to get out 2. Too big to carry 3. Need to set or assemble 4. Too heavy to carry
5	Bring		1. No way to transport

Notes: 1. Most of the time is spent in locating the item, and this is the most urgent issue needing improvement.
2. Everybody should know what everything is called.
3. Things need to be stored more efficiently.

5.4. DECIDING WHERE THINGS GO

Getting Rid of Things You Do Not Need

The first step is to cut inventories in half. The rule should be to have no more than one of any one part on hand at any given time. Any more than one is too many.

Determine the Analytical Method For Storage Stratification and Layout

There are some things that you will want to have close at hand and others that can be farther away. This is the kind of stratification that is needed. Do the things that are close at hand really need to be close at hand? In doing this, it is important to consider the layout of the entire building. Things that are frequently used might be better near the door. Heavy things should be where they can be moved easily. It is crucial in doing this stratification that you work within a systematic analytical framework.

Standardize Naming

It often happens that something will have two names: its real name and what everybody calls it. In such cases, make a decision which one you are going to use and make it stick. It only confuses people to have two names for the same thing. When you are getting rid of things is a good time to take inventory and see how many of each item you have. There may well be a lot of things that do not have a name. There may be times when two different things have the same name. There may be times when several things are called by the same name even though there are minor differences among them. Taking inventory will highlight all of these problems.

5.5. DECIDE HOW THINGS SHOULD BE PUT AWAY

Study Putting Away Functionally

Putting away functionally is, of course, that which is done in light of quality, safety, efficiency, and conservation considerations.

- There are many quality considerations depending on the features of the particular product, but the most important one is perhaps to be careful not to confuse things with different names. People are very prone to make mistakes with similar items.
- For example, if you have two twins side by side, it is very difficult to tell them apart. Likewise, things that look the same, have similar names, or have similar numbers should be placed some distance apart. Very often it helps to draw the outline of the tool on the tool board (see Photo 5.2), and different colors can be used to avoid any lingering confusion. Another possibility would be to have lines and a name panel, so that when you pushed the button by the name of the tool, a light would light up on the tool board by the tool you wanted (see Photo 5.3). It is also helpful to have the board and space number by the name of the tool. Anything that can be done to prevent mistakes should be done. (See Photo 5.4 and Figure 5.3.)

Names and Locations

Even if something does not have a formal name, there is bound to be some kind of a name that the people who use it know it by. And because everybody has a name (albeit sometimes a different name) for it, the lack of a name does not cause much confusion when people are working off on their own. How-

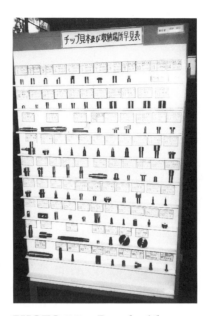

PHOTO 5.2.   Board with shadow outlines.

PHOTO 5.3.   Foolproofing retrieval.

PHOTO 5.4.   Safe storage.

ever, the lack of a common name can cause real trouble in team efforts, and it is essential that everything have a generally accepted name and that everybody knows what that name is. If it does not have a name, you cannot assign it a space and nobody will know where to find it.

- In doing your 5S activities, it is imperative that everything have both a name and a location. These names should be simple and easy to understand. They should also be reinforced, for example, by having them written on the tool boards and even on the tools themselves.

- In assigning storage space, designate not only the location, but even the shelf. Decide where everything should be, and make sure that is where it is. This is crucial.

- Item and location names go together. When the storage location is on the tool and the tool's name is on the storage location, you know you are making progress. Everything should have not only its own name, but the exact location where it is kept. (See Photo 5.5.)

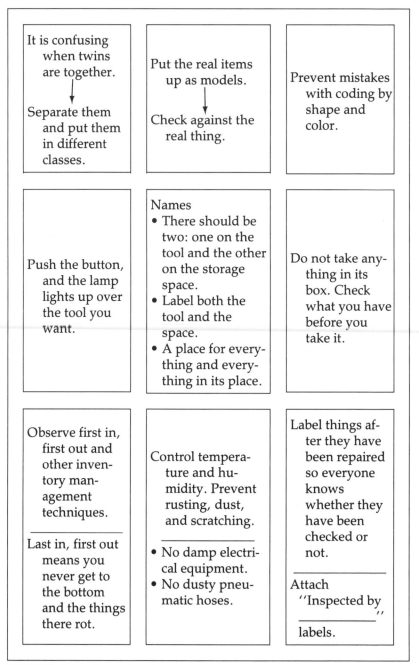

FIGURE 5.3.   Functional storage.

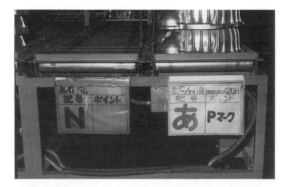

PHOTO 5.5. Labeling storage spaces. The signs indicate item names and location codes.

Making It Easy To Get Things Out and Put Them Away

- This entire process is intended to make the work go smoother, because when everything has a place and everything is in its place, there is less confusion and the work does go smoother. It helps to have diagrams and lights.

- It also helps if storage locations are not all over the place. Things should be where they belong and the system should be understandable, whether you have classified them by function, product, process, or whatever. (See Photos 5.6 and 5.7, and Figure 5.4.) It is especially important that sets and kits be complete and that spares be available.

- In designing storage facilities, heavy things should be on the bottom or on dollies so that they are easy to get at (see Photo 5.8). Other things might be hung from hooks, and the things that are used the most should be the easiest to get to.

- Having things readily at hand and easy to use means thinking about the job at hand. Most people find it easier to get things that are between knee and shoulder height. On the job itself, things should be within easy reach.

- It is important to take full advantage of all the storage space

PHOTO 5.6. Functional storage.

PHOTO 5.7. Storage drawer for specific parts.

Functional Storage		Storage by Product and Shop
• Storage by type of equipment, such that all similar equipment is together • Storage so the things you need most often are easiest to find • Spares are preassembled		• When some tools are only used with certain equipment, put them where they are needed. • Bits and other things can be stored ready to use.
Storage shelves for electrical equipment	Storage shelves for pneumatic equipment	Storage space for spares for _____ shop

FIGURE 5.4. Shelf stratification.

PHOTO 5.8. **Storing heavy
items—pumps on dollies.**

that is available. That means designing spaces to fit each
item. For example, long things demand special care. Hoses,
cables, and the like can be wound. Fan belts and other loops
can be hung. And little things might have to be in containers,
just as special boxes might be made for sets so you can be
sure they are all there.

5.6. OBEY THE RULES

Everyday Control and Preventing
Out-Of-Stock Condition

- When you look for something where it is supposed to be
  and it is not there, there are three possibilities: you are out
  of stock, somebody took it and has not put it back yet, or it
  is lost. But you do not know which possibility is true. Nor

do you have any way of knowing what you should do. If you are out of stock, have more been ordered or not? If somebody is using it, who is it and when will they bring it back? (See Figures 5.5 and 5.6.)

- Again, if it is out of stock, what is the procedure for ordering more? Are there any other stores or inventories around that might have some? Who do you contact? The ideal, of course, is that all of this would be clear at a glance. Every space should also have a note when to reorder (e.g., reorder when only five remain). There should be a note saying how to reorder, and even some reorder cards—preferably color-coded. In fact, many places have things so well arranged that when stocks get down to the reorder point, the reorder card is right there.

- In deciding how many to have on hand, the main question

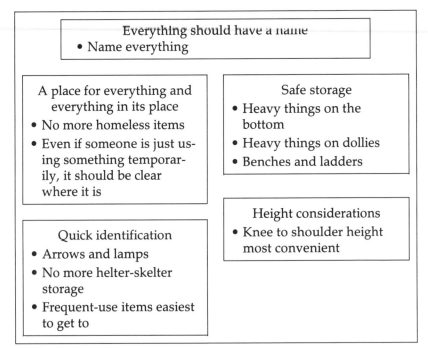

FIGURE 5.5.

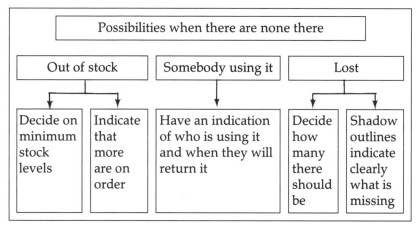

FIGURE 5.6.

is: How easy are they to reorder? If you can always get more in a hurry, there is no need to keep a lot on hand. If it takes a long time to get more, it would be wise to have spares. (See Photo 5.9.)

Reforming the Reorder Process

- Getting things out and putting things away can be a time-consuming process, and that is why we put things together in sets so that we can get everything done at once. Yet for frequent turnarounds or tool changes, where there are lots of possibilities and large numbers of things involved, it is important that procurement be fast and error-free. Many people find it convenient to have the things they use frequently right by the line, right at hand.

- Sometimes dollies are customized to carry the most frequently used tools or parts, and these can be fixed so that there is a clear distinction between the things everybody uses and the things just one process or person uses. It is important to make sure that the dollies are easy to move around and that they make the job easier to do.

PHOTO 5.9.   Shelves with lights to show
where things are.

Practicing Getting Things Out and Putting Them Away: The Benefits of *Kaizen*

Neatness is a process of eliminating the waste of time involved in getting things out and putting them away. But unless the results are tangible, it is hard to see what has been accomplished. Unless everybody practices getting it right, neatness is unlikely to have much impact. Happily, practice also tends to highlight the things that still need to be done.

Figure 5.7 shows the results that were obtained when getting things out and putting them away were made into a game. Changes and improvements were made on six common tools so that they could be retrieved and put away by anybody— from novice to veteran—even management. The best improvements are the ones that make it possible for anybody to do this. If this were an office rather than a machine shop, you could do the same thing with files. It should be possible for anybody to do this in half a minute or less.

5.7.   ITEMS TO REMEMBER ON PUTTING THINGS AWAY

Whenever you put something down, you should remember the following items, which are explained in what follows:

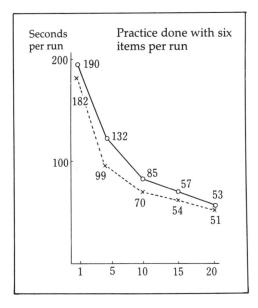

FIGURE 5.7. Storage and retrieval times.

- Outlining and placement marks
- Stands, shelves, and dollies
- Machine tools and other tools
- Blades and dies
- Materials and work in progress
- Contingency stocks
- Oils
- Instrumentation and measurement devices
- Large items
- Small items and consumables
- Labeling and display supplies

Outlining and Placement Marks

In starting neatness in a factory, the first step is to outline the passageways and to mark clearly where everything goes. (See

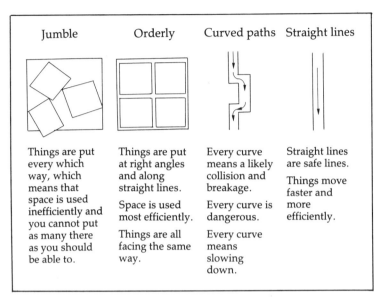

Jumble	Orderly	Curved paths	Straight lines
Things are put every which way, which means that space is used inefficiently and you cannot put as many there as you should be able to.	Things are put at right angles and along straight lines. Space is used most efficiently. Things are all facing the same way.	Every curve means a likely collision and breakage. Every curve is dangerous. Every curve means slowing down.	Straight lines are safe lines. Things move faster and more efficiently.

FIGURE 5.8.   Points to remember.

Figure 5.8 and Photos 5.10 and 5.11.) Of course, the first imperative is to design a layout that is conducive to good work, and this also applies to neatness as well.

The next imperative is to remember the straight-line, right-angle rule and the horizontal–perpendicular rule for layout.

PHOTO 5.10.   Well-marked passageways.

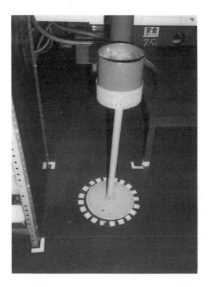

PHOTO 5.11. Placement marks.

These are important for getting the most out of your space, and it is also important for safety reasons that all passageways be straight lines. At the same time, this will give the factory a clean-cut look.

In many cases, it helps to have passageways along the walls, both to ensure that the main passageways are broad and uncluttered and to ensure that there are no dead spaces.

With the location marks for various things, it helps to create zones and to make sure that things are where they are supposed to be, because very often not having things where they should be has a detrimental impact on the work itself and can even upset the work process and hurt quality. Many offices have marks set up so that they are invisible when everything is where it should be but become visible when anything is out of place.

However this is done, it must be remembered that these lines and marks are clear decisions. Even just drawing the lines creates a more ordered feel to the workplace, and this is a very important step that cannot be neglected. Once the lines are down, of course, everyone should be responsible for seeing that things stay neat and clear and that nothing is outside its assigned boundaries.

In many cases, companies have found it helpful to use different colors for their main passageways and subpassageways. Color coding can go a long way toward making things easier to find and store.

Height limitations are also very important in deciding where to put things. Not only are such limitations important for safety reasons (to keep things from falling on people), they are also a good way to prevent the buildup of unnecessary supplies.

Drawing these lines and indicating where things go are all part of layout studies, and the three key considerations have to be (1) making the work go smoothly, (2) safety, and (3) a clean-looking layout.

Stands, Shelves, and Dollies

Stands and shelves are important to neatness, but too many stands and shelves can actually be an impediment to neatness. (See Figure 5.9.) Too much space is dangerous because it lulls you into thinking you have room for all these things. The first step at many factories is to reduce the number of stands and shelves. Once that is done, decide what absolutely has to be on a stand or shelf and throw the rest away. This is basic. Do not keep more than you need.

When your stands and shelves are all different heights, put some supports under them and make them the same height. Sometimes you will want to put casters under some so they can be moved more easily. You may want to make special stands that will hold just the things needed for a particular job. If there are frequent turnarounds or parts changes, you might have a stand with a set of the things you need.

Stands and shelves should not rest directly on the floor. Putting legs on them and getting them up off the floor makes it easier to clean and gives the place a tidier look. (See Photo

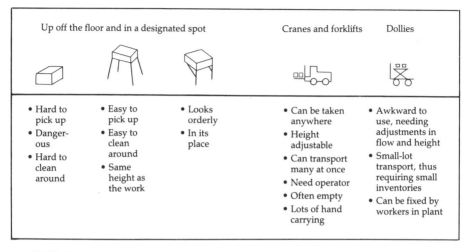

Up off the floor and in a designated spot			Cranes and forklifts	Dollies
• Hard to pick up • Danger-ous • Hard to clean around	• Easy to pick up • Easy to clean around • Same height as the work	• Looks orderly • In its place	• Can be taken anywhere • Height adjustable • Can transport many at once • Need operator • Often empty • Lots of hand carrying	• Awkward to use, needing adjustments in flow and height • Small-lot transport, thus requiring small inventories • Can be fixed by workers in plant

FIGURE 5.9.   Getting things off the floor.

5.12.) But that does not mean that you want a whole forest of legs.

Dollies are a means of conveying things from one place to another. Heavy things, of course, can be moved by overhead cranes or by forklifts, but if you rely only on cranes and fork-

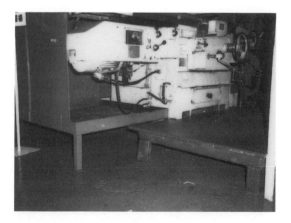

PHOTO 5.12.   Up off the floor.

lifts, people will end up carrying a lot of things by hand. At the same time, cranes and forklifts require special operators and usually are returned empty. Anybody can move a dolly, and dollies can carry much more than one person can.

The use of cranes and forklifts should be held to a minimum. Dollies are more efficient in many cases, especially because they can be designed for a multitude of uses. If you use a little imagination and make the dollies the same height as the workbenches, everything will be at the same height and you will not need to spend a lot of time lifting things and putting them down (see Photo 5.13). This will save both time and strain.

It is important to use your imagination and remember that the stands, shelves, dollies, conveyance chutes, and other things are all there to make the work go smoother, faster, and safer, to make cleaning easier, and for a host of other reasons. Feel free to innovate when it suits your purposes.

Wires and Ducts

There are all too many places that have multiple connections spreading out like a spider web (see Photo 5.14). There are also many that have cables buried under the flooring, snaking along

PHOTO 5.13.   Bench dollies.

Before

After

**PHOTO 5.14.   Wire management: before
and after.**

the floors, and even hanging from the rafters in an unsightly
jumble, where it is impossible to tell what is connected to what.
All of these are potential trouble spots prone to breakage, wear,
and error, leading to injury or machinery breakdowns. It is
imperative that policies be instituted to remove these wires and
ducts from underfoot, to bundle them, to label them, and to
make sure that all the lines are straight lines with right angles
and firmly anchored. (See Figure 5.10.)

   All of the buried lines should be dug up, put above ground,
and stapled firmly into place. Every line should be named and

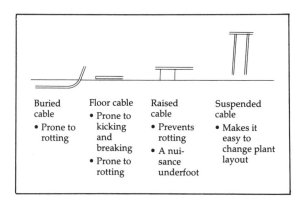

FIGURE 5.10.   Proper handling of wires and ducts.

numbered to prevent mistakes. And even the layout should be reconsidered and revised to facilitate moving things as necessary.

Machine Tools and Other Tools

Most factory work involves the use of machine tools, and there are great numbers of many kinds of machine tools. That is why it is so important that they be organized for easy use. The main points in this organization are

- eliminating the need for tools
- reducing the number of tools you need
- putting tools where you can get them right away
- putting tools in the order you need them
- putting tools so you do not need to change hands
- putting tools so you can put them away with one hand

Eliminating the Need For Tools

The best way to do this is to have the wrench permanently attached to the bolt head—to use wing nuts—or to use other techniques so everything you need is right there when and where you need it.

Reducing the Number of Tools You Need

If you can reduce the number of bolt sizes, that also reduces the number of wrenches that you need. You can also combine several tools into one like the Swiss Army Knife. It is also helpful to have a single tool such as an impact wrench with several different heads. (See Figure 5.11.)

Putting Tools Where You Can Get Them Right Away

The best place to put things is right where you are going to be using them. Of course, this means there is limited space and you have to cut down on the number of things that are there, but that is also a good idea. The best example of this is the way electricians use tool belts with everything they need. The same principle can also be applied by making just enough storage space near machinery to hold the tools for that machine. (See Photos 5.15 and 5.16.) And when you do this, it is a good idea to make space for a rag that people can use to wipe the machinery and keep it clean.

Putting Tools in the Order You Need Them

Assembly lines are set up to have the parts come in the order they are to be assembled. Even when you are doing an overhaul, it is a good idea to put things in the order you take them apart so that you do not forget anything when you are putting them back together. Just as people at formal dinners start from the outside and work their way in with the silverware, so should you have everything in order. Not only does it make it easier to find things, it ensures that you do not miss anything or get anything in the wrong order.

Putting Tools So You Do Not Need To Change Hands

One of the greatest wastes of time in any process occurs when people pick something up with one hand, have to change

Points to note	The company had been using circular steel panels for the pipe nameplates; these panels are bolted to the pipes.		
Improve-ments made	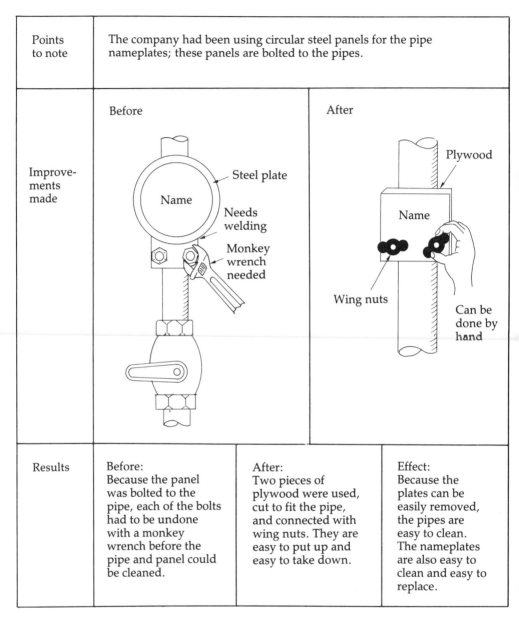		
Results	Before: Because the panel was bolted to the pipe, each of the bolts had to be undone with a monkey wrench before the pipe and panel could be cleaned.	After: Two pieces of plywood were used, cut to fit the pipe, and connected with wing nuts. They are easy to put up and easy to take down.	Effect: Because the plates can be easily removed, the pipes are easy to clean. The nameplates are also easy to clean and easy to replace.

FIGURE 5.11.   Reducing the number of tools you need.

PHOTO 5.15.   Tools conveniently stored.

hands to use it, and then have to change hands again to put it down. Eliminating this waste of time can radically improve efficiency, especially in manufacturing operations. This means putting tools on the right side of the person and in the right orientation to be used, and it means making sure that they are always ready that way. It means having enough room for the

PHOTO 5.16.   Things stored in an easy-to-get manner.

person to pick something up without a lot of tight maneuvering, and it means making sure that things are picked up in position and ready to go.

Putting Tools So You Can Put Them Away With One Hand

It is also a waste to spend a lot of time putting things away. Many people are being more efficient than they realize when they have chains on their glasses so they do not have to think about putting them away or wonder where they are. Wrenches can be hung up on hooks and hammers can even be hung in nooses.

It is crucial that the tools be put in good order and kept that way because these are things that are used over and over every day, and every saving is multiplied hundredsfold.

Blades, Dies, and Other Very Important Consumables

This is one of the most important quality points there is, and it is crucial that a system be created to maintain these things regularly and to ensure that they are in tip-top shape. (See

PHOTO 5.17. Making it hard to put things away wrong.

**PHOTO 5.18.   Storing tools so
the blades do not hit each
other.**

Photos 5.17 and 5.18.) There are a number of things to remember here.

- Create storage spaces so that it is clear what everything is and that protect these things from nicking, breakage, rust, and grime.
- Be careful that no filings, dirt, or rust gets into the tapered ends of the holders.
- Reduce the number on hand. Devise cases so that the blades do not hit each other or get damaged. Review sharpening and polishing procedures and the cases where things are kept. If there are any size changes, be sure to indicate that on the storage case.
- These items are very often stored vertically, so be sure to have a latch or other holder, as well as a cover for safety's sake.

Materials and Work In Progress
In Which the Numbers Change

It is very difficult to designate set places for things when the numbers keep changing. Even when you do, there is no assurance that they will always be full, and it is very likely that you will end up with space being wasted.

- For materials and work in progress, designate set places and decide how many of what should be there. Anything more than that is too many, and other arrangements should be made for this surplus. Even if they are put near the work being done, it should be understood that this is a temporary arrangement and there should be a clear decision on how long they will be there. When you have materials coming in or work in progress going out at regular intervals, with the result that things tend to pile up just before or after deliveries, there should be some space that is usually used for something else but is available to hold this overflow. Even so, the standing principle should be one of reducing the number of things on hand, and there should be a constant effort made in this direction. (See Photo 5.19.)
- At the same time, it often happens that work in progress,

PHOTO 5.19.   First in, first out.

**PHOTO 5.20.   Note how the
inclined bench ensures first in,
first out.**

finished products, and even just-in-case extras get a special
storage site and end up there for some time. The important
thing to remember here is first in, first out. Use that first
which you get first, and ship that first which you made first.
Do not create dead space where things pile up. (See Photo
5.20.)

- Other very important themes in quality control include that
  of ensuring that there is no damage to goods or parts in
  transit, that they do not get dirty, and that things are not
  mislabeled. In fact, these are the things that most production
  people are worst at, and they deserve close attention.
- Special space and special containers should be set aside for
  defectives and things that are pending a decision, and it is a
  good idea to color code these places and containers in bright

red or brilliant yellow and to label them clearly so there is no misunderstanding. And the containers for defectives should be small so they fill up quickly and call attention to themselves.

- Because the lack of even a single part can hold up an entire assembly process, it is important that all of the parts be there and that they be in order. Such process management is crucial. Many of the best factories have these things on small carts that are then lined up in order so that it is a simple process to do each step in order and to check that everything has been done.

Contingency Stocks

- In managing spares and contingencies, it is a good idea to know exactly how many of each you need and to know when it is time to reorder.
- And in managing these stocks, it is important to be very clear about their maintenance, including checking for nicks or scratches, rust, or grime. Printed circuits and the like should be stored so they do not bump each other and so they do not collect grime or dust. Very often, they need to be stored in a cool, dry place. (See Photo 5.21.)

PHOTO 5.21.   Storing fan belts.

Oils

The storage and maintenance of oils is another important point from the organization and neatness perspective. In doing organization and neatness, the procedures are as follows:

1. Consolidate the kinds of oils you use and cut down on the number of different kinds.
2. Devise color codes and special markings that will tell you both the kind of oil and how often it should be changed or added. And be sure to make this simple enough so that anyone can understand it and there are no mistakes.
3. Decide which oils are going to be in central storage and control and which are going to be substored and subcontrolled along the line. Then decide how much of what to put where along the line and what rules are going to govern resupply. Remember that this also includes designated storage space and containers, and that these things also need to be color coded.
4. Be sure to have all the tools you need, depending on the kind of oil, the way it is put into the machinery or applied, and anything else that is job-specific.
5. In addition to the production process itself, oils also need to be considered from fire, pollution, and safety aspects as well. Stop any leaks, and do everything possible to make sure that no dirt or other foreign matter gets into the oil.
6. Innovate to make it easier to pour the oil, even if this means installing longer-neck spouts or intakes.

Instrumentation and Measurement Devices

Some ideas for the storage of these devices are found in Figure 5.12.

- These things have to be accurate. Otherwise they are useless. It is assumed that they are checked regularly and adjusted

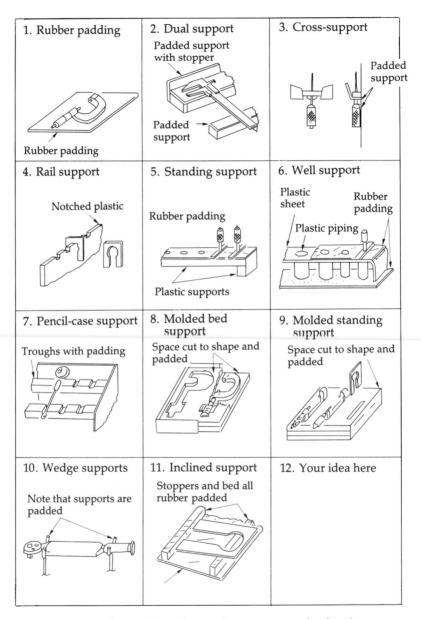

FIGURE 5.12. Some ideas for storing gauges and other instrumentation devices.

for accuracy, but this has to be clearly indicated. Of course, some things have to be more accurate than others, and this should also be clearly indicated along with the inspector's name. It is inexcusable that these should not be labeled or that the labels should have come off.

• When everyday maintenance is sloppy, these devices sometimes do not go back to zero when they are off, rusty, dented, or otherwise deformed. It is important to make sure that they do not get bumped around, dirty, or otherwise damaged. This is how you make sure that you are building quality in; and if they are off, your whole process is off. (See Photos 5.22 and 5.23.)

Large Items

Large items and heavy items are very individual, each with its own purposes and each used in its own way, and it is important to devise storage space and transport means for each and every item individually. (See Photo 5.24.) Because many of these items often have long cords, some way has to be found to wind up these cords and keep them from getting fouled. In addition, pumps and other heavy equipment have to be handled carefully and transported carefully for safety reasons as well.

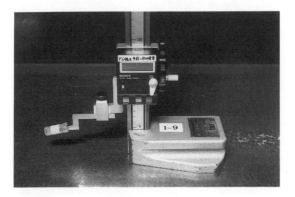

PHOTO 5.22. Cap protection.

PHOTO 5.23.   Storing gauges on sponge mats.

PHOTO 5.24.   Stored for easy use.

- Safety guards and cleaning tools have to be devised especially for each piece of equipment, and it is important that space be built for this equipment, where it is readily available but not in the way.

Small Items and Consumables

- Most of these items are maintained as everyday supplies, and the fact that they are used every day makes it all the more important that easy reorder procedures be devised.
- The problem arises when items fall into the line or get lost. That is why it is wise to keep the supply boxes only about 80% full and to have a clear line indicating where to stop, since having a little room to spare at the top will mean less risk of overflow or spillage. When things are put away, be sure to put lids on containers. Be sure to pick up any droppage and put it back where it belongs. Unless these items are picked up and put back right away, they will more likely than not either get thrown away (wasted) or mistaken for something else (resulting in lesser quality).
- A number of things should be supplied to the line in sets. These include springs and other items that are hard to handle, washers and other items that are difficult to pick up, bearings and fittings that are intolerant of grime, mold, or rust, and packings and gaskets that are ruined if they are broken, deformed, or even damaged. (See Figure 5.13.) Supplying them in sets also makes it less likely that anything will be forgotten. Ingenuity should be exercised to ensure that they are easy to handle, easy to install, and easy to get right.
- Although there are many things to remember in managing these small parts, it is also important to remember that storage is crucial and to devise ways to store each one suited to that particular part. Reordering should also be made simple and efficient.

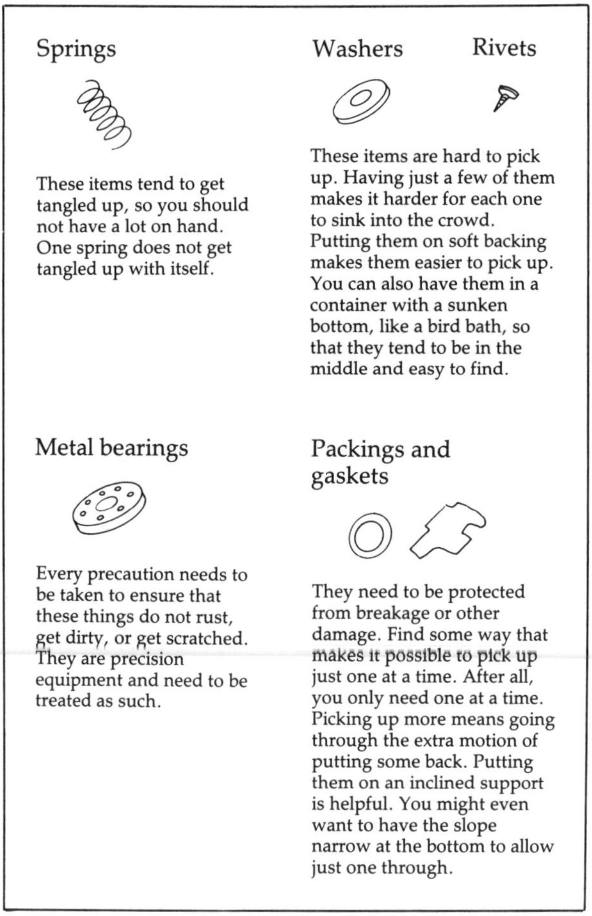

Springs

These items tend to get tangled up, so you should not have a lot on hand. One spring does not get tangled up with itself.

Washers   Rivets

These items are hard to pick up. Having just a few of them makes it harder for each one to sink into the crowd. Putting them on soft backing makes them easier to pick up. You can also have them in a container with a sunken bottom, like a bird bath, so that they tend to be in the middle and easy to find.

Metal bearings

Every precaution needs to be taken to ensure that these things do not rust, get dirty, or get scratched. They are precision equipment and need to be treated as such.

Packings and gaskets

They need to be protected from breakage or other damage. Find some way that makes it possible to pick up just one at a time. After all, you only need one at a time. Picking up more means going through the extra motion of putting some back. Putting them on an inclined support is helpful. You might even want to have the slope narrow at the bottom to allow just one through.

FIGURE 5.13.   Little things need special attention.

Labeling Supplies

Figures 5.14 and 5.15 show the main points to remember in putting up notices, posters, or signs, which include the following:

- Do not just put them up anywhere. Designate special places for them and stick to the designations.

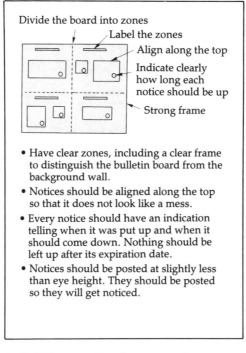

Divide the board into zones
Label the zones
Align along the top
Indicate clearly
how long each
notice should be up
Strong frame

- Have clear zones, including a clear frame to distinguish the bulletin board from the background wall.
- Notices should be aligned along the top so that it does not look like a mess.
- Every notice should have an indication telling when it was put up and when it should come down. Nothing should be left up after its expiration date.
- Notices should be posted at slightly less than eye height. They should be posted so they will get noticed.

FIGURE 5.14. Putting up notices.

- Be sure to indicate how long they are going to be up. Nothing should go up without an indication of when it comes down. (Not only are out-of-date posters a waste of space, they are up so long that nobody pays any attention to them anymore—and by extension, people get into the habit of not paying attention to any notices, even new ones.)
- Tape should be peeled off in such a way that the wall is not unsightly afterward.
- Notices, posters, and signs should be aligned along the top so they look neat.

Poster Paper

- There should be three or four standard sizes.
- Posters that are going to be hanging down should be care-

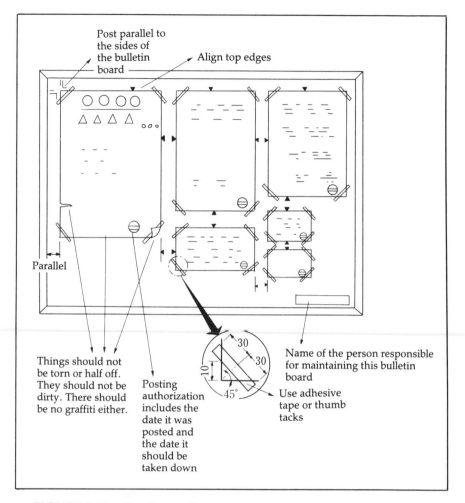

FIGURE 5.15. Posting notices.

fully measured first to make sure they are not going to be in the way.

- Posters should be put up firmly so that they do not blow around or fall down in the breeze when windows are open or when people walk by.

Lettering

- The messages may be handwritten, but they should be neat and legible. If possible, it is a good idea to use lettering sets. Important notices should not look like graffiti.

Stands and Signs

- These are very often a distraction. Heights should be carefully determined and placement should be carefully considered so that people can also see what they are all about.

Checklists and the Like

- Lists of operating conditions, procedures and instructions, checklists, and the like are important tools ensuring that a process is performed correctly. In effect, they are to the operator of a machine what the route map is to a bus or train passenger. Where are we now? What comes next? What do I have to do? And they should be designed so they are easy to understand even for someone who is not intimately involved in the process.
- Because these things frequently change, it is useful to have colored paper or flags at the key places, to have some means for people to check to make sure they are on schedule, and to keep them up to date.
- Numerically controlled (NC) machinery tape, of course, embodies all of these conditions and instructions, and it is essential that it be stored and maintained in the best condition possible—and that the limits on its use be spelled out clearly.

SUMMARY

- The very term neatness means getting things in order quickly and implies all of the procedures you need. As long as you are using things, you need these things around you, and thus there is much neatness involved in everyday life. Since changing hands and position are a major waste of time, you need to find ways to eliminate these steps. In some of the more disorderly shops, people spend a lot of time just wandering around looking for things.

- That is why you need to devise ways so anybody can find things easily and put them away where they belong easily. You might even turn this into a competition. For tools and documentation, people should be able to get them out and put them away in 30 seconds.

- It is important to devise efficient maintenance and storage, but that does not mean you can neglect safety and quality considerations. Set the allowable times depending on how often something is used and how important it is. This is also, when you think of it, a cost consideration. Stratify things by how much time and effort you want to spend on their management. Decide optimum stock levels for each item, but remember that the less the better.

- Neatness works best when everyone takes part and everyone exercises ingenuity in devising the storage means that work best.

Chapter **6**

Seiso = *Cleaning*

6.1. CLEANING THEMES

Cleaning Means Inspection

In the old days, when everything was in short supply and there was not much of anything, tools and machinery were kept spotlessly clean and treated with near reverence. Yet over time, as prosperity increased, people started taking a more casual, less caring attitude toward their tools and equipment. They developed a throw-away mentality. They started to think that it was cheaper to buy a new one than to fix the old one or even to keep it in good repair. This was reinforced by the hectic pace of modern life, in which the premium seemed to be more on time than on taking care of things. But even that is not the whole story.

More and more, cleaning and sanitation are viewed as part of the service sector—something you hire people to do. There are even a number of successful firms that have sprung up to cater to this mind-set. Laundries and dry cleaners are an obvious example, but there are also janitors who are hired especially to clean up after people. There are the "sanitation engineers" that populate modern business. There are people who make a living out of pollution control and waste disposal. There are even people who design and build what are called clean rooms. Cleanliness is big business now.

Related to many problems. Cleaning means more than just keeping things clean. It is more a philosophy and a commitment to be responsible for all aspects of the things you use and to ensure that they are kept in tip-top condition. You should never drift into thinking that cleaning is just cleaning and that it is tiring work at that. Rather, you should view cleaning as a form of inspection.

With the increasing sophistication of modern industrial products, dust, grime, foreign substances, burrs, and other problems are more and more likely to cause defects, breakdowns, and even accidents. Cleaning is the answer. Cleaning should be seen as a way of eliminating the causes of problems one by one, and it should be done in that spirit.

The Three-Step Approach

Very broadly speaking, there are three steps to proper cleaning. First is the macrolevel activity of cleaning everything and finding ways to deal with the overall causes pertinent to the whole picture. Second is the individual level, dealing with specific workplaces and even specific pieces of machinery. And third is the microlevel, where the specific parts and tools are cleaned and the causes of grime are ferreted out and corrected. (See Figure 6.1.)

Dealing with the causes has been explained in Chapter 4, so the main focus in this chapter is on the second and third levels.

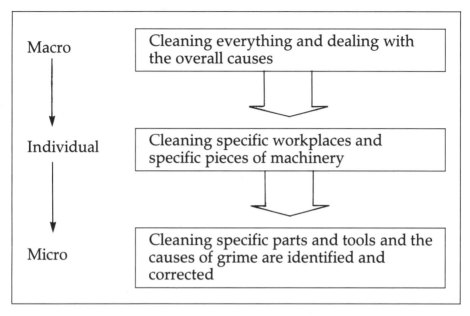

FIGURE 6.1. The three-step approach.

6.2. WORKPLACE AND EQUIPMENT CLEANING

Procedures

There are four steps (see Figure 6.2) that should be followed:

1. Divide the area into zones and allocate responsibility for each zone.
2. Decide what has to be cleaned, decide the order, and then do it. At the same time, it is important that everyone fully understand the importance of cleaning so that you can analyze the sources of the problems.
3. Revise the way the cleaning is done and the tools used so that those hard-to-clean places will be easy to clean.
4. Decide on the rules to be observed to keep things looking the way you want them to.

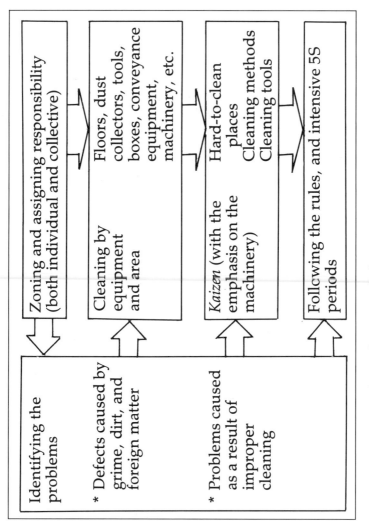

FIGURE 6.2. Promoting a cleaner workplace.

Zones and Responsibility

In allocating responsibility for the 5S activities, it is wise to start first with group responsibility for specific areas. Then you can make this a group responsibility with one person as the group leader. Yet this alone is not enough. Everybody talks about the group doing things, but this seldom works in the long run. Just look at the conference rooms or toilets at your company. Groups are only collections of individuals, and groups cannot do anything that their members do not do.

Rotating responsibility. Everyone keeps his or her own car clean, and everybody is careful not to get any scratches on it. But when it is somebody else's property—especially when that somebody else is an impersonal entity such as the company— people all too often let things get a little dirty or a little rusty. Joint responsibility means that it is everyone's responsibility, but that also all too often means that it is no one's responsibility. Many companies try to get around this by having the responsibility rotate among the members of the group. This might be a daily rotation intended to spread the responsibility. In rotating responsibility for the type of job that no one especially likes handling, a person when finishing his or her turn would ensure that the job is passed on to the next person.

Unless there are clearly delineated individual responsibilities and a spirit of cooperation in taking care of the group's responsibility zone, it is impossible to hope for good teamwork. In this, cleaning is very much like the zone defenses mounted in team sports such as soccer or football. You are going to lose the battle against grime unless everyone plays to the best of his or her ability.

Graphing individual responsibility. In 5S activities, it is best to work from the assumption of individual responsibility as much as possible with the understanding that people will help each other on the really difficult parts.

For example, you might start by graphing out the individual areas of responsibility. In doing this, it is important that all assignments be absolutely clear and that there not be any undefined, unassigned, or gray areas. (See Figure 6.3.)

Unless each and every person takes these admonitions to heart (see Figure 6.4) and accepts personal responsibility, you are not going to get anywhere.

Implementation

If you do the cleaning in an orderly progression by piece of equipment and by location, you are bound to discover a lot of

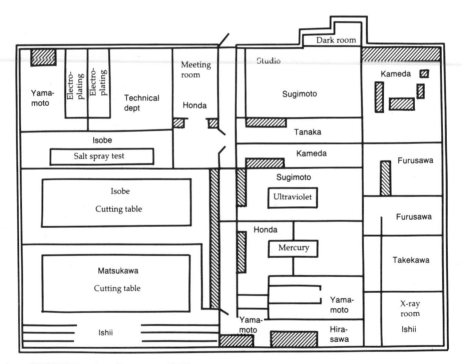

FIGURE 6.3.   Responsibility map.

- I will not get things dirty.
- I will not spill.
- I will not scatter things around.
- I will clean things right away.
- I will rewrite things that have gotten erased.
- I will tape up things that have come down.

FIGURE 6.4. The 5S pledge.

problems in the process. That is why it is good to do this in tandem with your annual housecleaning and facility *kaizen*.

Some of the problems that you are likely to encounter in this process are shown in Table 6.1.

Among the many places that you should be cleaning in this process are ceilings, electrical equipment, ducts, air-conditioning filters, inside and all around machinery, boxes and shelves, dollies and other transport equipment, and protective covers. These are all places that will have an impact on your process and hence on your quality.

TABLE 6.1. Problems discovered in the cleaning process.

- Dirty air-conditioning filters lead to defects in printing.
- Filings in the conveyance chutes lead to scratching.
- Scraps in the die lead to faulty pressings.
- Things fall off the equipment and get into the products.
- Things get dented or bent in conveyance.
- Filings and other particles contaminate the resin.
- Dirty coolant leads to clogging.
- Dust and other substances ruin the paint jobs.
- Bad connections are made because the electrical contacts are dirty.
- Fires are caused because garbage shorted the electrical equipment.

Operation handkerchief.   This can go by many names—one-wipe strategy, operation cleanup, and more—but it is fundamentally a campaign to get everyone to do a little cleaning and polishing. (See Photo 6.1.) And if you do this with white rags, it is also possible to display these rags, both to indicate the places that need cleaning the most and to show how, after a while, even the dirtiest places are not as dirty as they used to be.

Cleaning machinery.   At first, people ran around the plant with home vacuum cleaners, but this soon proved to be inefficient and better equipment was devised by attaching vacuum cleaners to the forklift trucks. (See Photo 6.2.) This does not have to be special cleaning equipment if you use your imagination, but some places have devised cleaning robots and keep them running around the plant all day.

Facilitating the Process

Three-minute 5S activities for all.   This means having everybody engage in 5S activities for a very short time—just 3 minutes a day—every day. The important thing is to make sure

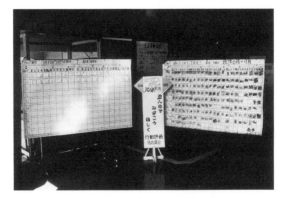

PHOTO 6.1. Operation handkerchief.
Wipecloths before (r.) and after (l.) a 5S
campaign.

PHOTO 6.2. Cleaning machinery.

everybody is doing the same thing at the same time—that everybody is taking part. This is very difficult to do, and it involves lots of precoordination, leadership, and some way to involve the laggards.

But it is not only slack-offs. Sometimes the instructions are not clear and the whistle (if you use a whistle) is not loud enough. (Anything less demanding and less piercing than a whistle, and the participation rate is even lower.) But it is important that everyone take part in the same activity at the same time. Everyone has a good reason for not taking part, and all of these good reasons have to be overcome if the 5S activities are to succeed.

Importance of limiting the time. There is no reason the 3-minute 5S activities have to be for exactly 3 minutes. The important thing is that it be for a short time, but it could just as well be 2 minutes or 5 minutes. The important thing is that this be for a clearly defined time and that the time be used to best effect. And because it is for such a short time, it can be approached not as 5S activities, but as part of the daily routine. People can do this as part of their work. If they do not correct the sources of cleaning difficulties, they will find that their work does not go as smoothly and that their efficiency is down. (See Figure 6.5.)

• The places that are the hardest to clean will be the dirtiest.
• Improve the cleaning process and tools so you can do the cleaning quickly.

FIGURE 6.5. Hard-to-clean places.

There are all kinds of variations. There are 1-minute 5S activities. There are 3-minute 5S activities. There are 10-minute 5S activities. And there are even 30-minute 5S activities. In fact, you can have combinations of these. The important thing is to decide clearly when they are going to take place and what people are going to do during this time. They could take place at the beginning or at the end of work. They could take place at the end of the week or at the beginning of the month. It is good to have variety here with different periods assigned to different tasks. If everybody pitches in, you will find you can get an amazing amount of work done in 3 minutes. Three minutes is about as long as a popular song. It is not that long, and it is important that it end when it ends.

For example, you might decide to set aside 3 minutes at the start of the afternoon. And once the 3 minutes are up, start the line. This does not mean putting things away when the 3 minutes are up. It means doing the quality and safety checks at 2 minutes and 30 seconds so that everything is ready to go when the 3 minutes are up. If you have said this is going to be 3 minutes, do not make it any more or any less.

Everyone at once helps quality and safety. Having everybody work on the same thing all at once is extremely helpful to quality and safety checks. Some places have found that simply instituting a policy of having everyone do the same thing several times a day every day has drastically reduced the number of mistakes made on assembly operations.

6.3. ELIMINATING EQUIPMENT DEFECTS AND DOING TOOL CLEANING (EQUIPMENT 5S)

Cleaning and Inspection

Equipment 5S is the first step to self-maintenance. Although this means detailed cleaning and inspection of the equipment and tools, it does not mean that people just start looking at whatever is close at hand. The problem areas have to be identified and analyzed first, and decisions have to be made on how certain things are going to be cleaned and inspected. It is even a good idea to think about the little defects that might be discovered so people will know what to watch for.

Inspection checklists.   Cleaning and inspecting equipment means peering inside, and this means taking off all covers, filters, and other things that keep you from getting a good look at the interior. Even just taking off these things is likely to turn up a number of problems. Yet, this is not going to be all of the problems. Unless the people doing the cleaning and inspection have a good grasp of the equipment's technical intricacies, they will not know what they are looking at and will be unable to perform the kind of inspection that is needed. And even the most expert inspectors should use checklists so they do not miss anything. (See Figure 6.6.)

Checking the basics.   There are many aspects to machinery and equipment—including pneumatic lines, hydraulic lines, lubrication, the electricals, and the mechanicals—but the inspection should be looking for those basic factors that determine wear and aging in equipment. That means checking for grime and making sure that the cleaning is thorough. That means checking to make sure that equipment does not run out of oil and lubrication. That means making sure that everything is tight and nothing is so tight that it is bent out of shape. And that means checking for overheating and making sure that temperature control is maintained.

In going about this, it is sometimes good to designate a model area that gets the full treatment. Not only does this experience highlight any problems in the procedures, it also demonstrates how easy or hard the work is and serves as a standard. (See Figure 6.7.)

Cleaning and Inspection Education

There are a number of things that people have to learn before they start the cleaning and inspection that are so essential to equipment 5S activities.

Cleaning	Illustration
Equipment • If there are parts that get dirty every day, they should be cleaned every day. • In cleaning moving parts, be sure to stop the equipment before you start the cleaning.	
Moving parts • Clean these with clean rags—and never with air blasts. • Air blasts can blow grime onto the surfaces and create friction. Air hoses can also blow grime into people's eyes.	
Oil gauges and meters • These should be cleaned so that you can always see how high the oil is and what the meter reading is.	
Limit switches • Clean off all grime and dirt. • Remember to stop the equipment before you start the cleaning.	
Photoelectric sensor lenses and the like • Wipe gently with a soft rag to avoid scratching.	

FIGURE 6.6. The key points to a good cleaning job.

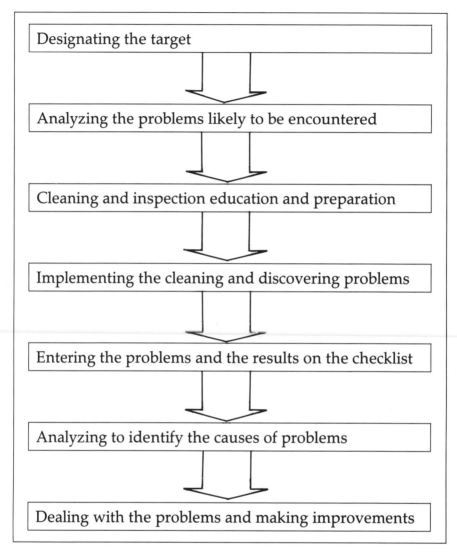

FIGURE 6.7.   Promoting equipment 5S's.

Functions and Structures

The first thing is that people have to learn the functions and structures of the equipment they are going to be working on, and they have to gain a full understanding of the mechanisms involved. Each piece of equipment works in its own way to do its own job according to its own principles, and anyone who does not understand the equipment cannot possibly know what is important and what to concentrate on.

At many companies, it turns out that not even the people who have used the equipment for a long time understand how the equipment works or what it really does. Many companies are so interested in getting people to operate the machinery that they only tell them how to do that and do not bother with these more important "non-essentials."

Internalizing Equipment Knowledge

In doing the cleaning and inspection, easier is better, and this demands one more round of education about the equipment to make sure that people really understand what it is all about. Where are the filters and how do they work? Draw the lubrication system, including where the oil is poured in and what valves it goes past on its way to where. There are all kinds of questions that can be and need to be asked. How many of what are there? Where do you check for oil leaks, and where might the oil be coming from? Where are all the electrical connections?

For smaller pieces of equipment, people should be working on the actual equipment itself. It is also helpful to go back and find a defective sample and ask people what might have caused the problem. People need to do more than understand the equipment. They need to think about it and identify with it.

Doing Cleaning Inspections and Discovering Minor Defects

When you actually start this process and take off the covers and other protective panels, you will discover all kinds of problems.

Figure 6.8 shows just some of the problems that were discovered at one company when the production and maintenance people cooperated on a comprehensive cleaning and inspection.

Grime and clogging because of inadequate cleaning.   For one thing, there was a lot of grime and clogging attributable to cleaning inadequacies. Places that were ordinarily out of sight were hence out of mind. There were also a lot of oil problems,

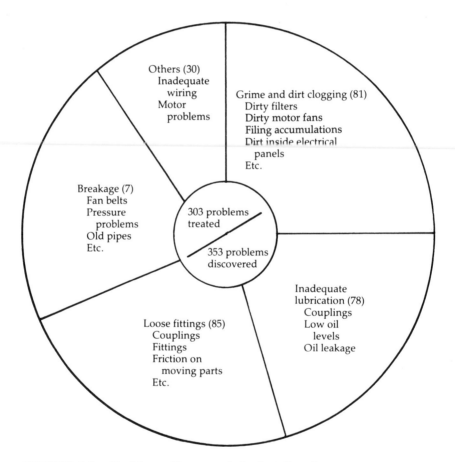

FIGURE 6.8.   Problems discovered during cleaning.

especially in places that normally were overlooked. There were also loose places that concealed real problems but were untreated because people figured it was enough to tighten it up once more.

Technicians often say that they hate to hear something bump inside a piece of equipment and that they want to build equipment that does not make thumping noises. But it is not the noise per se that they object to. Rather, it is the cause of the noise—the loose bolt that means something else works loose and smashes into another part with reverberations that spread like ripples on a pond.

They are concerned that a loose part in one place will later mean a loose part somewhere else and that this will eventually create major breakdowns. That is why they want to get to the cause of the problem right away and fix it. Even if it is just a single bolt, they know the dangers that this loose bolt poses, and they do not take such things lightly. As a general rule, people only find between 5% and 20% of the loose bolts.

Finding problems reinforces confidence.   There should be several people spending several hours on the cleaning and inspection of a single major piece of equipment. And you should be prepared that they will find 50 or even 100 or more problems. These are little misorientations or defects that do not turn up in the daily inspections. There will be so many of them that everyone will be amazed. In fact, people will be amazed not only that there are so many problems, but that they had been blithely using the equipment, unsuspecting and unknowing. But once they discover these problems, they will have more confidence in what they are doing.

Cleaning-Inspection Points For Most Equipment

Although you will need a detailed and exhaustive checklist for each piece of machinery, it is possible to mention some of the main items common to most equipment. Here they are listed by aspect.

- Cleaning: Grime, clogging, dustballs, rust, leakage, etc.
- Oil: Running out of oil, running low on oil, leakage, filter clogging, dirty oil, dirty or bent oil lines, clogged drainage ports, worn or torn packing, etc.
- Tightening: Loose bolts, welding detachments, loose parts, vibration or bumping noise, movement in shock absorbers, friction, etc.
- Heat: Oil tanks, motors, heaters, axles, control panels, washing or cleaning water, cooling water, etc.
- Breakage: Breakage, chipping, meters that do not return to zero, cracked glass, handles that have come off, broken switches or buttons, cables or bundles of wires that have come unraveled, things that are misshapen, etc.

The equipment aspects that you should be inspecting for can also be classed by function or even location. (See Table 6.2.)

- Pneumatics: Air lines, air valves, connections, meters, adjustors, filters, air leakage, etc.
- Hydraulics: Inside the hydraulic oil tanks, oil valves, filters, adjustment devices, pumps, hoses, gear boxes, gauges, cylinders, etc.
- Mechanicals and power trains: Motor fans, fan belts, couplings, joints, pulleys, chains, pumps, etc.
- Electricals: Control panel covers, control panel interiors, lamps, light bulbs, toggle switches, etc.
- Tools and measurement devices: Tools, bits, blades, measurement devices, gauges, dies, etc.
- Equipment-specifics: Fire bricks, rollers, flues, latches, chutes, transport equipment, etc.

Analyzing Why

Every piece of equipment fulfills specific functions, and understanding these functions will make you a better inspector. This

TABLE 6.2.   5S self-evaluation sheet.

Step 1. Identifying problems	Division: Name:	Section:	Dept:	Team: Circle:	
Item	Evaluation criteria			Points	Subtotal
Moving parts	1. Are the oil level gauges easy to read?				
	2. Is there any slippage or other strange noises from the motors, belts, transmissions, clutches, chains, etc.?				
	3. Are all the safety covers on tightly?				
	4. Is the tension right in all the belts?				
	5. Are the cooling fans clean?				
Hydraulic and pneumatic parts	6. Is there any oil leakage from the pumps, valves, etc.?				
	7. Are the right pressure gauges being used? Are they working right?				
	8. Are all the oil inlets capped?				
	9. Is all the pneumatic equipment being used correctly?				
	10. Are all the pipes and clamps tight?				
Electricals	11. Do all the meters, etc., have warning labels showing their limits?				
	12. Are there any burned-out bulbs?				
	13. Are all the switches free of oil, water, and grime?				
	14. Are all the machinery parts in good working order and firmly attached?				
	15. Are all the cables firmly but flexibly attached?				
Nuts and bolts	16. Are all the nuts and bolts tight (M10–280 kg/cm being the standard torque)?				
	17. Are there nuts and bolts in all attachment holes?				
	18. Are there 2–3 threads visible beyond the nuts?				
	19. Are all the adjustment bolts tight?				
	20. Are wing nuts used wherever there is vibration?				
Remarks				Overall ranking	

Note: Rank from 1 to 5 (5 being excellent, 3 average, and 1 poor)   Date:

understanding can be vastly enhanced if you ask yourself why for each of the problems and minor defects that you identify. Ask yourself:

1. Why is this important?
2. Why has this been overlooked or ignored?
3. What can be expected to happen if we leave this the way it is? What impact will it have? What are the principles and mechanisms involved here?
4. Why has this gone so long before being detected? What could have been done so that it would have been detected earlier?
5. Why is it this way? Does anybody know about this? Does everybody know about this?

By constantly asking yourself the whys and whats, you will get to the core of the problem and will be able to involve the small-group quality circles as well as management in finding and implementing solutions. Inspections are all well and good, but they are not the end of the process. The purpose of an inspection is to find problems and then to solve them so that they do not show up on the next inspection.

SUMMARY

- Cleaning is one of the most basic 5S activities, and it would not be far off the mark to think of it as the essence of the 5S. This is not a new idea. It is something that has been around for a long time, but it is no less important for its lack of novelty.
- Cleaning includes both cleansing and polishing. And both of these activities are important to making us better people. Even if the cleaning is done on specific pieces of machinery and equipment, the very cleaning process itself requires considerable long-term dedication and patience. It has been said that there is no job that does not involve cleaning.

- It is also true that cleaning is inspection. Cleaning is a process that treats each piece of machinery, equipment, or tool as important in its own right and seeks to take proper care of it. Once this is understood, it will be realized that the careful cleaner is also the most thorough cleaner and is hence in the best position to spot minor problems while they are still minor. As such, cleaning is also a process of detection and correction.
- Understanding something inside out the way you do in a cleaning and inspection routine also opens our eyes to the broader world outside of our workplace. Recently, people have taken to quantifying the degree of cleanliness in the realization that this is crucial to safety and quality. The drive in many companies now is for zero grime and zero dirt.

Chapter 7

Seiketsu = *Standardization*

7.1. STANDARDIZATION COMES FROM 5S MAINTENANCE AND CONTROL

Standardization means maintaining a state of cleanliness, which, in the context of the 5S's, includes other considerations such as colors, shapes, clothing, and more that give a sense of cleanliness.

However, for the sake of discussion in this chapter, standardization will be considered simply as the repetition of organization, neatness, and cleaning and as a constant awareness and activity to ensure that the 5S status is maintained. This means regularizing the 5S activities so that abnormalities show up, and exercising ingenuity in creating and maintaining visual controls.

7.2. MAKING ABNORMALITIES OBVIOUS WITH VISUAL CONTROLS

Because it is people who control and manage things, it is essential that your people be able to tell the difference between normality and abnormality and be able to act accordingly. Yet, as

137

seen in industrial defect rates, the possibility of abnormalities occurring is generally 1% or less, and most of the time things will be operating as normal with no problems. It is in the midst of this normality that people must identify abnormality.

Anybody can spot an abnormality. These abnormalities are very often things that the person who is not looking for them will miss, but that someone who is alert and attentive will spot. If the person is not assuming that everything is okay until it blows up and if the person is constantly asking if this or that is okay or if there is a problem, then he or she will be able to spot most abnormalities. That is why it is so important that the person be so alert and look for abnormalities.

And, at the same time, that is why it is important to exercise ingenuity so that abnormalities are more visible and so that anybody who is paying close attention can point them out. In effect, this is a process of ensuring that abnormalities surface. It is important that they be visible to anyone.

Visual management is being alert. How can you best make sure that abnormalities surface? In our everyday work, we use our minds to remember things and all five senses to do our best work. What is important here is to transform these static senses into dynamic awareness and to make them come alive for us. And it is the visual sense—the sense of sight—that is the most important. It has been estimated that 60% of all human activity starts with sight. Of course, we also learn from our sense of hearing and our sense of feel, and it is also important to make the fullest possible use of these senses as well, but it is our sense of sight that dominates. That is why visual management is sometimes referred to as the embodiment of visual awareness.

7.3. TRAINING A CHILD IS ALSO VISUAL MANAGEMENT

Making the rules easy to follow. Japanese mothers spend a lot of time correcting the way their children's shoes are placed in the foyer and telling their children to put their shoes the right way (neatly side by side with the toes pointed toward the door). But no matter how many times you tell them, some children never seem to learn. As a result, some mothers have come up with the idea of putting shoe placement diagrams on the floor, and their children have picked the idea up so quickly that they even take care of guests' shoes. No explicit threats were needed. No long lectures. Just the shoe diagrams on the floor. And this is the essence of management.

In the same way, if you want the people in your plant to follow the rules, you have to devise tools that make the rules easy to follow. People find it much easier to do things if they have some kind of actual guidelines, and such tools also make it easier to standardize.

7.4. HIGHLIGHTS OF VISUAL MANAGEMENT

The following briefly summarizes the highlights of visual management and makes them easier to visualize:

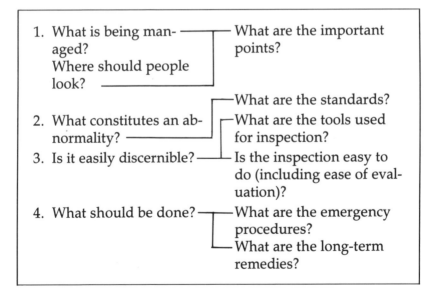

1. What is being managed?
   Where should people look? — What are the important points?

2. What constitutes an abnormality? — What are the standards?
   What are the tools used for inspection?

3. Is it easily discernible? — Is the inspection easy to do (including ease of evaluation)?

4. What should be done? — What are the emergency procedures?
   What are the long-term remedies?

7.5. EVERYTHING IS IMPORTANT

It is important that people be vigilant and hawk-eyed about everything. In a jet fighter plane, for example, there are lots of special markings, color codings, and numbers on the hull and in the engines. There is a special symbol to indicate where the gasoline inlet is, special marks to indicate where it is safe to stand, colors to indicate electrical systems, little lines indicating how tight a bolt is supposed to be shut, torque numbers for bolt tightening, and many, many more. These devices have been thought of to ensure that the fighter plane is capable of top performance anytime, anywhere.

People too are replete with such markings. When they are tired, they might massage their temples. When they are sick, they run a temperature and develop whitish hues on their tongues. The human body has its frailties, but it also has its own monitoring system to signal us when something is wrong. These are the places we have to watch, and we have to be on the lookout for abnormalities.

Ingenuity to provide that extra measure of control. Although we usually speak of these trouble spots as demanding special attention, the truth is that these are not things that everybody readily understands. And like the human body, your factory equipment usually has covers on it that conceal the crucial innards. So it is essential that you exercise ingenuity to make it possible for people to peer inside the equipment, as it were, and to evaluate what is going on. Unfortunately, all too few companies are exercising this kind of ingenuity and initiative. And all too often these companies are not exercising the kind of management control they need either. It is enough to make you wonder what management does on its daily inspection tours.

Yet even within this, there is some very good work being done on safety management. There are warning signs in bright red or brilliant yellow. There are very clear warnings on what to be careful about and what equipment is particularly dangerous. And these signs are posted where they are sure to be seen. Would that it were the same way with equipment mainte-nance. There are numerous important parts and functions that need to be checked. There are numerous functions that need 5S attention. There are many, many places where visual control is needed.

7.6. TOOLS AND METHODS FOR VISUAL CONTROL

It goes without saying that you need to use visual aids in visual control. You need to exercise ingenuity in devising creative tools to facilitate this process. Of course, it would be a mistake to rely on visual cues alone and you also need to use the other four senses in helping people get a total grasp of what is hap-pening.

To give some idea of the kinds of visual control displays that are needed, there are, for example:

- displays to help people avoid making operating errors
- danger alerts
- indications of where things should be put
- equipment designations
- cautions and operating reminders
- preventive maintenance displays
- instructions

The main points in creating such visual control displays are listed in Figure 7.1. If you will think of these things when you create and revise the standards and the tools that people need to identify abnormalities, you will find that the work goes smoother and the output is better.

Standards on Right and Wrong

In conducting visual management, it is important to distinguish clearly between right and wrong and to have clear standards that

1. Make them easy to see from a distance.
2. Put the displays on the things they are for.
3. Make them so that anyone can tell what is right and what is wrong.
4. Make them so that anybody can use them easily and conveniently.
5. Make them so that anybody can follow them and make the necessary corrections easily.
6. Make them so that using them makes the workplace brighter and more orderly.

FIGURE 7.1.   Points to remember in making visual control tools.

anyone can understand. In addition, the standards should be visually displayed and based on visual cues that make it possible to identify the problem when there is trouble. These should be simple things, like the shoe patterns on the floor.

Perceptual Tools

Very often, the problem is a complex technical problem. In such cases, you do not need diagnostic tools that will enable anyone to come in and fix things. What you need are tools that will enable anyone to come in and tell you that something is wrong. You need warning lights or the equivalent so that people will notice that there is a problem in the making. These are your visual control tools, and these are the sorts of things you should be thinking about.

Making Inspection Easy

In most cases, the really important parts—the parts that you need to manage most thoroughly—are buried deep within the equipment or system. To make things worse, these are usually the same places where the grime piles up. This means they are very difficult to inspect. You need to clean them up. You need to make them easier to inspect and manage. You need to make major improvements, concentrating on these parts. You need to make it so that it is possible to manage these parts with a single look.

7.7. VISUAL MANAGEMENT MANUALS: 5S STANDARDIZATION

So that everybody can get it right. Unless you standardize, everybody will be doing things his or her own way and making assessments based upon his or her criteria. For example, even with 5S activities, there are some people who assume that the 5S's automatically mean getting out a broom or a dust cloth. These are people who do not stop and think about why something is done, much less why it is done the way it is. For these people, you need to standardize what is to be done, what is to be maintained, what to do in case of emergencies, and everything else. You need to standardize, and you need to explain the thinking behind the standardization. And then you need to practice and practice so that everyone can do things right. And the reason you need to do all of this is that the modern workplace demands that each and every worker be able to manage his or her own work responsibly. (See Photo 7.1.)

At the same time, you need to be careful that this does not degenerate into a game. The stickers and labels that you put up are not just decoration. People have to think about exactly what needs to be said where and why so that they can do an accurate diagnosis and be sure that they know what is happening. Unless people are thinking, they may end up putting a temperature label on a motor fan cover, using terms that only they understand, and doing other things that create more problems than they solve. (See Figures 7.2 and 7.3.)

7.8. COLOR CODING

There have been some major changes in Japanese factories over the last few years. Young people today come right out and say

**PHOTO 7.1.   Visually understandable
weekly work schedule.**

that they do not want to do dirty labor, and they do not answer
the help-wanted ads for grimy factory jobs. It is easy to say
that today's young people have become soft, but people spend
the better parts of their lives at work, and there is no reason
why they should be doing something they do not like. Rather
than criticizing today's young people, it is more important to
do what you can to make sure that the factory is a bright and
cheerful place to work.

Some factories now have relaxation areas complete with
aquariums, plants, and other things that help people wind
down. There are also air-conditioned factories. Corrugated iron
roofing has given way to modern architecture. Factories that
used to be no more than shacks are now modern buildings
complete with soundproofing, dust collection, and innovative
lighting. But for all of these changes, the most remarkable
change has been in the way color is used.

Indispensable color coding.   It used to be that both factory
machinery and work clothes were brown or gray because these
colors do not show the dirt much. It was almost like military
fatigues—factory camouflage. Now people wear white or other
light colors and the dirt shows up immediately. Now the machinery is pale pastel colors. Heavy machinery is just as color-

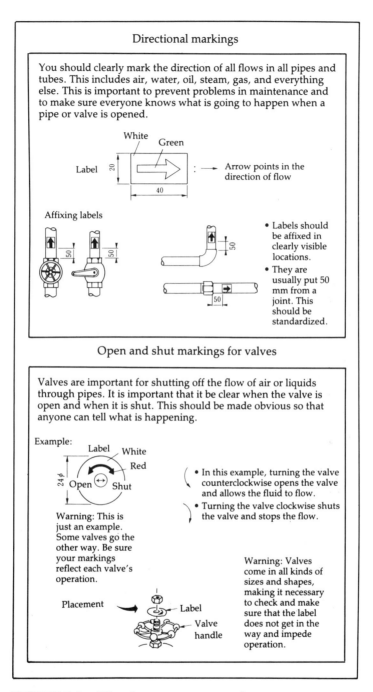

FIGURE 7.2. Visual management made easy.

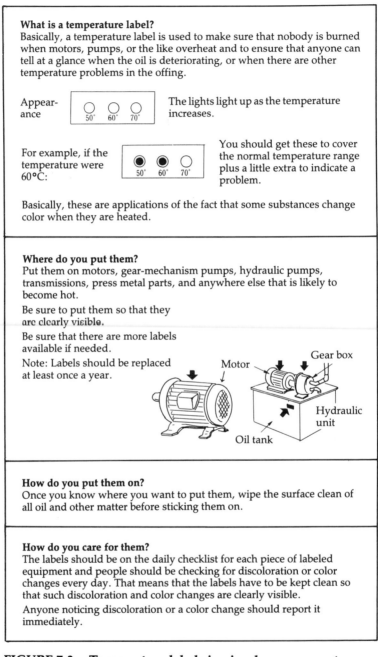

What is a temperature label?
Basically, a temperature label is used to make sure that nobody is burned when motors, pumps, or the like overheat and to ensure that anyone can tell at a glance when the oil is deteriorating, or when there are other temperature problems in the offing.

Appearance   [50° 60° 70°]   The lights light up as the temperature increases.

For example, if the temperature were 60°C: [50° 60° 70°]   You should get these to cover the normal temperature range plus a little extra to indicate a problem.

Basically, these are applications of the fact that some substances change color when they are heated.

Where do you put them?
Put them on motors, gear-mechanism pumps, hydraulic pumps, transmissions, press metal parts, and anywhere else that is likely to become hot.

Be sure to put them so that they are clearly visible.

Be sure that there are more labels available if needed.

Note: Labels should be replaced at least once a year.

Motor

Gear box

Hydraulic unit

Oil tank

How do you put them on?
Once you know where you want to put them, wipe the surface clean of all oil and other matter before sticking them on.

How do you care for them?
The labels should be on the daily checklist for each piece of labeled equipment and people should be checking for discoloration or color changes every day. That means that the labels have to be kept clean so that such discoloration and color changes are clearly visible.

Anyone noticing discoloration or a color change should report it immediately.

FIGURE 7.3.   Temperature labels in visual management.

ful as home appliances. Now the factory is a rainbow of color.

The floors and walls that used to be bare concrete have now been painted in bright colors. Companies that used to use whatever was cheapest are now ordering expensive paints to create a brighter work environment. And they are finding that people are more careful of the paint jobs and that they actually last longer as a result, meaning that the more expensive paint is cheaper in the long run.

Indeed, many companies have adopted "official colors" that they use on their trademarks, machinery, stationery, and other places to give the company a uniform identity. These are bright, clear-cut colors to convey a bright and clear-cut image. Colors are recognized as an important part of corporate identity campaigns.

At the same time, colors play an important part in such management campaigns as safety campaigns, quality campaigns, and the like. Soft colors can be just as effective as vivid or loud colors. It is all a matter of making the color fit the job.

7.9. APPROACHES TO COLOR

Preparation means effectiveness. When it comes time for painting, many people think this means painting everything in sight. They decide that the purpose is to make everything look better by painting it, and so they go heavy with the paint. Sometimes they even paint things that are better left unpainted—things such as oil spouts and pressure valves. Painting is more than painting. A lot of preparation has to be done first. You have to scrape and sand off the old paint, and make sure you have clean surfaces that are ready for the paint. Then and only then can you start painting.

All of this preparation takes both time and money. But if you do not do the preparation, you will end up wasting time and money. Painting also takes time and money, and it is important that you make the necessary preparations so that it is efficient and effective. Prepare the surfaces. Decide exactly how you want things to look. Are there any tricky surfaces that will demand special painting techniques? Are all of the safety, fire, and other regulations met? Do you have enough of each color? There is much that has to be done before you can lay down that first layer of paint.

By yourselves if you possibly can.   When it comes time for painting, there is a great temptation to call in an outside contractor. This temptation should be resisted. It is far better if you can do the whole job with your own people. After all, you are the people who will have to do the retouching if there are chipping, scratching, or other problems later. You cannot call in an outside contractor for every little touchup, and people will feel more proprietary about the work if they have done it themselves. Not only will people learn a lot about painting, they will also identify with the workplace and take more pride in how smart it looks if they have done the work. (See Figure 7.4.)

Painting the floors is a much bigger job than painting the walls or ceiling. The floors are the final repository of most of the factory's grime and dirt. As such, they are usually the dirtiest places. At the same time, they are very likely to be scratched and marred because everybody walks on them, pushes carts and dollies on them, sometimes even drives forklifts on them, and puts all the shelves, equipment, and everything else on them. Yet when all is said and done, painting the floors gives a new sparkle and élan to the workplace.

Not only are floors difficult to paint, they are nearly impossible to maintain. Yet it is essential that the effort be made and that you do what you can to keep the floors looking freshly painted. If they get dirty, mop them. If they get chipped or scratched, do a touchup paint job. Paying attention to these little things is how you pay attention to the big things.

7.10. METHODS OF VISUAL MANAGEMENT

Labels

In managing equipment it is important that it be labeled with both name and use. This applies to everything.

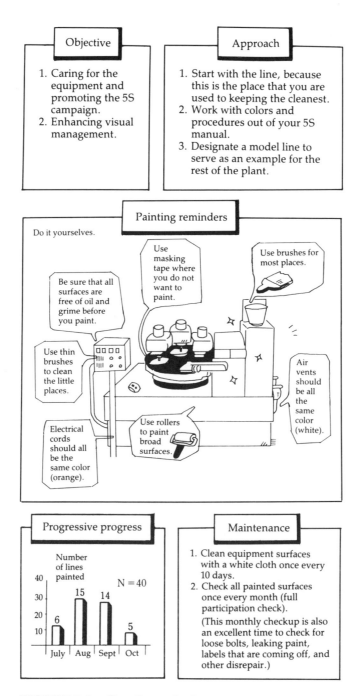

FIGURE 7.4. Creative painting.

Lubricating oil.   This is one of the easiest to understand items, and each container needs to be labeled with the type (grade) of oil, the color, and where it is for.

Precision management labels.   These should show the degree of precision, the management level, and the cycle period. (See Photo 7.2.)

Annual inspection labels.   This is basically the same as the inspection sticker on your car showing when it needs to be inspected. The labels should be attached to all equipment so that you do not miss any inspections. (See Photo 7.3.)

Temperature labels.   There are many things that you can do to indicate heat levels, including special labels and colorings. Some of these things fluctuate with the temperature and others hold the highest temperature registered so that you can spot momentary problems even if you do not happen to be there at the moment.

Responsibility labels.   These labels should show who is responsible for what. Everybody should be responsible for some-

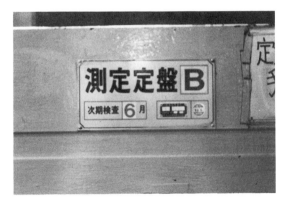

PHOTO 7.2. Precision management label indicating measurement standard and next calibration date.

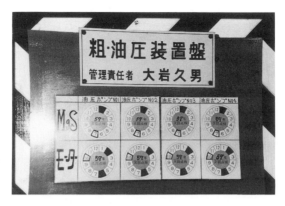

PHOTO 7.3. Monthly inspection label indicating item, person responsible, and inspection cycles.

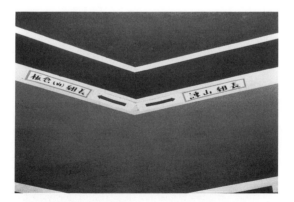

PHOTO 7.4. Assigning responsibilities. The corner is the dividing line separating areas of responsibility between two different persons.

thing, and everything should be someone's responsibility. The best way to make this very clear to everyone is to attach responsibility labels. (See Photo 7.4.)

Other labels.   Among the many other labels that you will want to use are those indicating what things are and drawing attention to special safety considerations.

Limits To Management

Labels are a good way to highlight the limits to management visually.

Zone labels on meters.   On every meter, there should be clear indications of what the normal values are and where the danger zones are. (See Photo 7.5.) These should be clearly labeled, perhaps emphasized by color coding. The same principle applies to inventories, and there should be some visual indication when it is time to reorder.

Okay marks.   By putting lines on the machinery and on bolt or screw heads, you can indicate clearly when the bolt or screw

PHOTO 7.5.   A properly labeled meter.

PHOTO 7.6.   Transparent covers facilitate inspection.

is tightened properly. At the same time, misalignment provides a quick visual clue that it is loose. This same principle applies to all kinds of things. You will be surprised at how many things can be marked as okay with a simple line or arrow.

Position marks.   It is a good idea to have little position marks for where things go. Even on television, they have marks that tell the announcers and other celebrities where to stand. Surely you can do the same for your equipment (and for the people who might have to move it). Place footprints where people should stand. Place marks on the floor to indicate danger zones. Place lines to indicate where things are supposed to stop. Put up lots of visual clues so that everybody will be able to see what is happening and to anticipate what will happen next.

Visual Ingenuity

Transparency.   In most factories, things are put in lockers, on closed shelves, and under covers to keep them out of sight. But this is all too often like sweeping things under the rug. Out of sight, out of mind. Those closed spaces are often among the most disorderly places there are—because they are not a constant eyesore. So it might be a good idea to take the wraps off these messes. Make the covers transparent. If you must have metal panels, put inspection windows in them. Make it so everybody can see what is happening and how good (or bad) things look. (See Photo 7.6.)

Visualizing conditions.   Many places put little ribbons on the fans so you can see the breeze. As a variation on this, they put windows and plastic strips in some of the drain pipes so you can see the effluent flowing. There are many other things you can do to help people visualize what is happening. (See Photo 7.7.)

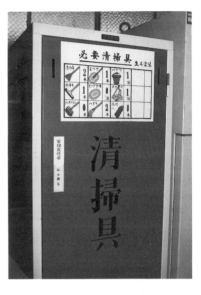

PHOTO 7.7.   Making conditions visually understandable.

PHOTO 7.8.   Show what is inside.

Trouble maps.   When there are problems, diagram them on a map of the shop. Just as many sales departments have pins in maps to show where their people are, you can also have pins to show problems, emergency exits, fire-fighting equipment, and other important locations. Put the maps where they are visible to everyone. In a reverse sense, a trouble map can also be an "excellence zone map" for workplaces and processes that are trouble-free.

What is where?   Just as you need to know where to find tools when you need them, you also need to know where to find people. You need a chart of who is where and how to get them (telephone extension numbers for some, special beepers for others). When people are away from the workplace, you need to know where they are and how long they are going to be there. And, of course, this is also true of equipment. If some-one has checked it out, you need to know who has it and for how long. (See Photo 7.8.)

Quantification. By constantly measuring things, quantifying the results, and analyzing the data statistically, you can quickly identify the limits to management and spot deviations before they become major headaches.

SUMMARY

- Unlike the other terms, standardization suggests a state of affairs. It is what you get when you have concentrated on organization, neatness, and cleaning over and over again.
- Asked how to maintain this state of cleanliness, some people will talk about personal hygiene. Even when you put it in personal terms, it is clear that you need set routines (standardization) and constant effort to maintain a state of cleanliness. Accordingly, you also need creative management and visual reminders to help everyone be constantly aware of the whys and hows of standardizing cleanliness.
- Visual appeals are among the most effective tools at your disposal. That is why it is so important that you be unrelenting in visual management.
- What constitutes a deviation? How did it happen? What has to be done as a result? The answers to all of these questions have to be clearly obvious in visual form. And when possible, you should also appeal to the other senses as well.
- The 5S's are easy to do once. It is constancy that is difficult. It is the repetition that is hard. Yet this constant repetition is essential and is the only alternative to backsliding. That is why visual management is so important—so everybody will know right away when there is a problem and you will be able to keep things the way they should be.

Chapter 8

Shitsuke = *Discipline*

8.1. DISCIPLINE AS A WAY OF CHANGING HABITS

The good teams play by the rules. Whether it is in the work-place, in the military, or on the playing field, team activities are cooperative activities. Everybody has to be working together, thinking together, and acting together to make a strong team. And the more demanding the work, the more important this is, because even the slightest mistake can mean failure. The rules are strict, and everyone is careful to do what he or she should.

In steelmaking, shipbuilding, construction, and other in-dustries, for example, teams assemble half an hour before the work starts so they can suit up and get ready mentally for the job that lies ahead. People working on assembly lines also know that one person can delay everyone if he or she is late or makes a mistake, and that is why both workers and line supervisors alike are so intent on getting things right.

People by their very nature have a tendency to slack off—

witness the prevalence of flash-in-the-pan 3-day wonders—and verbal promises tend to be forgotten or overlooked. At the same time, people tend to fall into an unthinking routine, forgetting why they are doing what they are doing and just going through the motions. That is why you need rules. That is why you need teamwork. That is why you need to keep everyone thinking and on his or her toes.

People make mistakes. Computers do exactly as they are told, but people tend to make mistakes. For example, if you tell someone to copy a 500-word text, odds are he or she will make two or three mistakes. And with sophisticated systems, there are all the more possibilities for making mistakes and the mistakes are all the more serious. When the little mistakes that people make come together, you have quality problems and reliability problems—which means you have customer dissatisfaction and market problems.

These things tend to compound. Even if you have 99.9% reliability on each step, this falls to 91% when you have 100 steps. Just as you would fix a machine that became old and started malfunctioning, so should you be attentive to the likelihood that your people are going to start malfunctioning and need to be maintained from time to time.

Doing the right thing as a matter of course. Discipline is how you practice and practice so that people do the right thing naturally. It is a way of changing bad habits and creating good habits. And the 5S's cannot succeed without discipline. If you want to do your job efficiently and error-free, you have to work on this every day. You have to pay attention to the little things. You have to plug away patiently, developing the right habits. You have to have an orderly workplace where everybody knows what is expected and does it.

8.2. HABIT FORMATION

It is not that difficult to get into the habit of doing what is expected of you.

- Standardize (systemize) behavior if you want good results.
- Correct communications and training makes for assured quality.
- Arrange it so that everybody takes part and everybody does something, and then work on implementation.
- Arrange things so that everybody feels responsible for what he or she does.

  People should verbalize their responsibilities each day, and they should act on them.
  And when they make a mistake, it is important that management point this out and make sure it is corrected.

  ↓

- This is how you institutionalize good practices, and this is how you create a disciplined workplace.

  ↓

- Everybody working together makes for a stronger team and a stronger company.

If you just follow these simple procedures, it will be possible to manage and maintain even the most sophisticated system and to keep it running smoothly.

8.3. WHY COMMUNICATION FAILS

Telephone. There is an old game in which the first person whispers a message to the person next to him, she whispers to the person next to her, and so on down the line. The message does not need to be that complicated, but people are always surprised at how garbled it can get with even just half a dozen repetitions. People tend to hear what they expect to hear—to adjust the sounds unconsciously to fit their perceptions and expectations. This becomes even more pronounced when the message is somewhat vague or confused to start with.

The difficulty of clear expression. It has even been suggested by some people that humans are inherently uncommunicative and that it is human nature not to communicate clearly. We often complain that people do not do what they are told, but there is some question as to what they have actually been told and what they think they have been told. Many is the quarrel that has started with, "He said . . . " and "I did not." And many is the time when a person only half-listening says, "Uhh," and it is taken as active agreement.

The importance of reconfirmation.   Given these human frailties, how can you ensure that you do communicate and that everything is understood? The only way is to talk things over—to make sure it is a two-way conversation—and to make sure that what was said was understood right then before mistakes crop up. Reconfirmation is the key. You need both the initial communication and then the feedback on what was received.

Everybody has to be open to what other people are saying and has to learn to be a good (which means accurate) listener. Just as you use visual aids to help people see things better, you can devise audio aids to help people hear better. This is all part of better communication. (See Figure 8.1.) It is no accident that so many 5S manuals are full of pictures, charts, and other visuals to help readers understand what is happening, and it is no accident that people are increasingly turning to video tapes and other instructional aids that have sound tracks.

8.4. FOLLOWING UP ON STANDARDIZATION AND CHECKLISTS

When an inspection is not an inspection. Checklists are very commonly used maintenance tools, but they can also contribute to the very problems they are supposed to prevent. Somebody who goes down the same list every day, checking this item and that item as okay very easily slips into the habit of assuming that all of the items are actually okay.

Marking them okay becomes a routine that replaces the

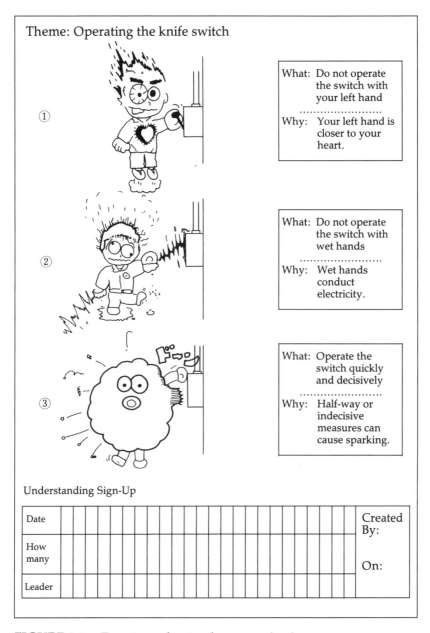

FIGURE 8.1.   **Easy to understand communication.**

work of checking to see if they actually are okay. Even if there is something amiss, he or she is lulled into missing it and marking the item okay. And this is compounded when management signs these checklists without really looking at them.

Inventing ways that force the checkers to be reliable.   It is important to remember that, for many checkers, their job is to make correct and accurate entries on the checklist so that management and supervisory personnel can see how things are going without actually going to the workplace. Looking at the checklist should be the equivalent of touring the plant. It is not that people cannot believe the checker without a checklist or that the checklist is itself inherently more trustworthy. Rather, the checklist replaces having to ask the checker a lot of detailed questions.

Thus, the trick is to design the checklist so that it includes all of the necessary information and so that the person has to fill it out right. And this means going back to the 5S rules and introducing visual controls. (See Figure 8.2.)

All the points that have to be checked should be listed. And if the checker is alert, you do not really need a checklist. The reason you have a checklist is to make sure nobody forgets anything. This does the same thing. There is no need for the checker to remember everything, but the reminders tell him or her exactly what to look for without being lulled into doing it on autopilot. This is a supplement and a prod, and there could well be another list (a data sheet) to enter data readings.

On-site training.   If the supervisory personnel are to be able to ascertain whether or not things are as they should be—to exercise visual control without actually going to the workplace floor and looking at the actual equipment—it is essential that the following points be emphasized to the people who do the actual checking.

- Why does this same place have to be cleaned and inspected time after time? Have the functions and structures been thoroughly studied and the causes identified?

		Things to do	
		Manufacturing	*Administration*
Three-minute 5S		1. Check your own clothing. 2. Check for any leakage or droppage, and pick up any parts, work, trash, or whatever that is on the floor. 3. Wipe the temperature labels, position markings, and other important places with a rag. 4. Wipe up any water, oil, or whatever that may have spilled or leaked. 5. Realign anything that is out of place.	1. Check your own clothing. 2. Check for any leakage or droppage, and pick up any parts, work, trash, or whatever that is on the floor. 3. Straighten your desktop. 4. Check where your desk and filing cabinets are and fix them if they are out of place.
Five-minute 5S activities		1. Clean up the plates and labels and make sure they are clearly legible. 2. Wipe the main places on the machinery with a rag. 3. Make sure all of the bits and tools are where they should be. 4. Get rid of anything that is not needed there.	1. Get rid of things you do not need or personal effects in your desk drawers. 2. Check where the filing cabinets, bookcases, and other furniture are and fix them if they are out of place.
Ten-minute 5S activities		1. Wipe the key parts and other places on the machinery with a rag. 2. Fix any labels that might be coming off. 3. Clean the floor. 4. Get rid of the trash in the trash bins. 5. Check the labels, instructions, and oil inlets, and fix anything that is amiss.	1. Get rid of anything that you do not need that is on top of filing cabinets, bookcases, and other furniture. 2. Fix any labels that might be coming off. 3. Clean the floor. 4. Check to see that the files are numbered, in proper order, and all accounted for. 5. Check to see how many pencils, erasers, and other things you have.

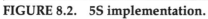

FIGURE 8.2.   5S implementation.

- Is it easy to clean and inspect? Are things easy to see? Is it easy to identify abnormalities?
- Is there anything else that could be done to make things even easier to see and understand? Would it be possible, for example, to consolidate things by working from the inside out?
- Are these functional parts so clear that anyone can understand what is happening?
- Is everyone proud that all of the functional parts are always clean?

Of course, these things that should be asked about the main functional parts are just the highlights of the cleaning inspection and are intended to ensure that the cleaning inspection is done right.

The importance of the creative process.   The process of creating standards and checklists is very important. Standards should be produced with the full participation of all the people who will actually be using them, and checklists should be produced in the process of actually checking the equipment. They should not be handed down from on high. Rather, they should be practical, detailed standards and checklists that can also serve as instructional materials. They should be real-life standards and real-life checklists. And things that are done regularly should be put on the 5S calendar.

8.5. PRACTICE UNTIL YOU CAN DO IT UNFAILINGLY

Practice is the best learning.   Just because people say they understand something is no guarantee that they really do— much less that they are able to do it. In technical training, it is essential that the process be explained, that people be shown how to do it, and that they be given the opportunity actually to do it themselves. These are all essential steps. Unless the person actually tries it, you have no way of knowing whether or not the person can actually do it. "Try it" is more than an invitation. It is a mandate.

For example, if you are doing turnaround on a machine, it is important to make sure that the person can go through all of the steps and can go through them in the time available. People who are new to a process typically take twice as long to do it. People who are new to a process typically make more mistakes. And as a result, they have to redo things and all of this adjusting and correcting takes even longer. Likewise, because they are not sure what comes next, the work does not flow smoothly.

Earlier, it was noted that people have a great propensity for forgetting. Even professionals—golfers, pianists, and others—practice every day. They know that no matter how good you are, you need to "stay in practice."

If this is true for things that people do every day, it is all the more true for emergency procedures such as fire drills and earthquake drills. If you do not practice the procedures when you have time, the fumbling and mistakes can be fatal in a real emergency. Everybody has to understand fully what is involved, what has to be done, and how to do it. Practice, practice, and more practice.

8.6. PERSONAL RESPONSIBILITY

With today's modern equipment, each and every worker makes a difference. Defects are the result of a process gone bad, but there is no point in just pointing at the defects if you do not make an effort to correct the causes. Are people following the standard operating procedures? Is everything the way it should be in the workplace?

Asking these questions immediately raises the question of how you can tell if people are following standard operating procedures and if things are the way they should be. This you do by checking the readings from the meters, by checking that the right materials are being used, and in other ways. But the clearest indication is by looking at the results of the process—

the product. If people are following standard operating procedures and if things are the way they should be, you can reasonably expect that the output will be good. (If output is better when people are not following SOP, you need to change your SOP.) And following these procedures is the individual worker's responsibility. (See Figure 8.3.)

It is often said that everything will be all right if everybody just does what he or she is supposed to, but that is much harder than it seems. It is not so much that people intentionally deviate from the standards, but that they forget what the standards are and why. They make careless mistakes because they are in a rut or because they are thinking of something

			Name:					
Motto: Streamlining for straight-line processes								
			Results					
Item	My responsibilities	Target	Oct	Nov	Dec	Jan	Feb	Mar
Quality	Check initial, intermediate, and final stages so that nothing is rejected in the inspection.	Zero defects per month	0 0 0 0	0 0 0 0	0 0 0 0			
Production	Modify the tools so that there is less turnaround time, with the final goal being straight-line processing.	Get one process down to straight-line processing every quarter	0 0 0 0	0 0 1 0	0 0 0 0			
Maintenance	Conduct daily and other regular inspections so that there are never any surprises.	Zero surprises per month.	0 0 0 0	0 0 0 0	0 0 0 0			
5S's	Maintain the 5S's in my area, and constantly strive to make things better.	80% or better at Level 5	85 90 95 90	100 95 85 90	95 95 100 100			
Safety	Eliminate careless accidents (being especially careful of fingers in putting things down).	Zero injuries per month	0 0 0 0	0 0 0 0	0 0 0 0			
Act as soon as you discover anything amiss.								

FIGURE 8.3.   A typical individual responsibility checklist.

else. You need to foolproof your procedures as well as your equipment.

Starting with the easy parts. Discipline is a matter of internalizing the rules. It means having each person pledge to do his or her job right. It means having each person reiterate his or her responsibilities to himself or herself. And it is best here to start with the simple things. People should verbalize what they are doing as they do it. And the practice should start with practice in remembering.

Some plants have my-responsibility campaigns with full participation by everyone. Managers are responsible for the results, but workers are responsible for the process. Everyone has important responsibilities, and everyone has to be aware of his or her responsibilities.

Changing things from time to time. Although the people who are doing the work should be responsible for devising the list of their responsibilities, it is also important that they have direction from time to time—direction that might even include changes. This list can be made up as the person goes through his or her process, and it can either be posted someplace in the workplace or printed on a small card that the worker carries.

But the fact that the worker has a card does not mean he or she should rely on the card. Everyone should know his or her responsibilities by heart. Everybody should be able to do everything on the list any time and get it right every time. To make it as clear as possible, it is a good idea to divide things into quality, production, maintenance, safety, 5S, and other categories. From time to time, there might even be spot checks.

Whether you are talking about managing by objectives, personal-responsibility campaign, or whatever, discipline demands that

- each person's responsibilities be clearly delineated
- people be given practice in fulfilling responsibilities
- people be mathematically literate

8.7. RULE-OBSERVANCE CAMPAIGNS

Practice is the best way to ensure that people are able to do what they are supposed to on a daily basis. Although the daily routine should be a constant reinforcement of good habits, all too often the daily routine is a dulling experience that takes the sharp edge off of people's abilities.

That is why it is important to designate specific themes for practice sessions and to have everybody practice the same thing. See if you cannot find some way to make a game out of it—at first for fun and then as a competition. Even if people already know how to do something, practicing it this way will refresh their memories and hone their skills.

Some of the things that you might try are as follows:

- Stranger in the night: A way to reinforce remembering who people are and the civilities of a kind word.
- Whistle clean: Having everyone start cleaning when the whistle blows and then seeing how clean things are when it blows again X minutes later.
- Pick up: A game in which teams compete to see who can find and pick up the most trash.

SUMMARY

- Discipline has more than an ethical dimension. It also means thinking about the many problems that occur from day to day, resolving to do better next time, and going through the rigors of doing better. This is especially important when it comes to quality, safety, and pollution considerations. Is that valve really shut? Is the safety switch on? People sometimes make the most unbelievable mistakes because they let their guard down—because they forget their discipline.
- As long as we have to rely upon people (ourselves included),

it is essential that we do what we can to enable people to work better and smarter. This involves more than reading books and attending lectures. It means instruction, practice, and more practice. It means internalizing what you are supposed to do and why.

- Yet it is very difficult for people to do the same thing properly over and over. By their very nature, people are fallible. People are all too prone to slip into the easy way of doing things rather than the right way. When you assume that something is easy just because you have done it thousands of times, that is when you are most likely to get it wrong. That is why it is so important to practice, because practice reinforces correct habits. That is why it is so important to be strict about how things are done—even the little things.
- In many ways, creating a disciplined workplace is the most important thing you can do to ensure product quality.

Chapter 9

The 5S's in the Office: The Office as a Paperwork Factory

9.1. APPROACHING THE 5S's IN THE OFFICE

A Factory By Any Other Name

Office work is management's job, and it is just as important that this be done functionally and effectively as it is that factory work be done functionally and effectively. The accounting department, for example, has to do the monthly tallies clearly and accurately. They have to get the numbers out quickly and in a form that will give top management a clear picture of where the company is headed.

Accordingly, the office needs the 5S's to eliminate inefficiencies, to prevent mistakes, and to keep things running smoothly. And when you think about what has to be done to raise efficiency and to foolproof the work so that anyone can do it and anybody can understand what is being done, it is obvious that the office is basically the same as the factory. They both get raw materials and turn out a product, the only difference being that the factory deals in things and the office deals in information. (See Figure 9.1.) As such, it should also be obvious that the same 5S principles can be applied to both factory and office.

Issues In Office Work

The things that complicate office work are that there are greater individual differences, that it is outwardly harder to standardize, and that it often appears inscrutable to outsiders. In addition, much of it is done by hand with wide discretionary latitude, such that it is difficult for other people to fill in or help out.

Often there are no or only minimal standard operating procedures, working conditions vary widely, and it is not a very mechanized process. There are no written standards. There is no foolproofing. All in all, office work is still in a very primitive stage as far as the 5S's go.

Even though the office is producing information, this is usually used in house rather than sold to outside customers. There may be some requirements as to who is supposed to produce what information by when, but there is very little monitoring along the way to ensure that everything is going smoothly and that no mistakes are being made. And as a result, there is very often little awareness of the need for *kaizen* and for the 5S's.

9.2. MAIN POINTS IN OFFICE 5S ACTIVITIES

The office is overdue for the 5S's, and the main points of 5S activities must be

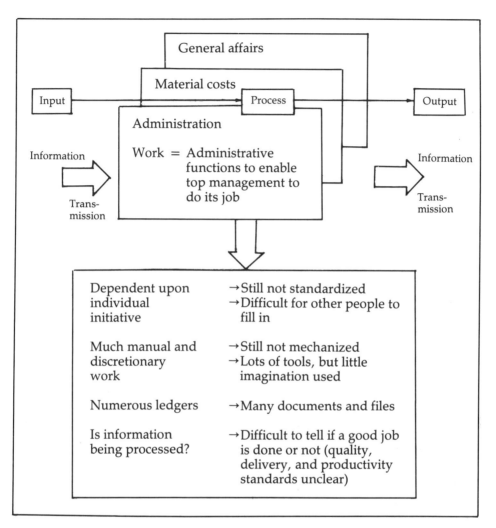

FIGURE 9.1.   Characteristics of office work.

1. Reducing the number of ledgers, forms, tools, and the like to eliminate all the unnecessary clutter.
2. Pulling out all the paperwork, files, tools, and the like and finding better ways to store things. People should be able to get anything they need in 30 seconds. You should start a "one-is-best" campaign to get people to write memos no

longer than one page, to have things kept in just one place, to have just one form for things, and to eliminate the idea that everyone has to have his own copy of everything.

3. Shifting from the individual-based to group-based work. Standardization and support systems (e.g., multifunctional people) are needed to even out the work load.

4. Organizing and implementing *kaizen* so that your ingenuity yields tangible results (the five W's and the one H). Make planning tables showing such things as what the plan is, how it is supposed to be implemented, and how much progress has been made. By breaking the progress down into separate steps, it should be possible to standardize and hence to create manuals detailing how each step is to be performed. There should also be a space to evaluate what is happening, since this will enable you to identify the trouble spots.

5. Studying and improving office tools. Very few of the tools and ledgers that people use in the office were designed for that specific office. There is thus considerable room for customization and improvement. Paperwork, ledgers, and tools should be created around the job, not the other way around. Many times, you may even find that the best way to improve a form is to eliminate it. Use your imagination, and aim for tangible results. (See Figure 9.2.)

6. Trying for a clean and orderly office. The office is the first place many visitors see. It shapes their first impressions. It sets the tone for the company. Yet that is just one reason why it is so important that you make a total effort to make sure that the office is clean and orderly—meaning that there is no grime or trash on the ceiling, the floor, the walls, the desks, the filing cabinets, or anywhere else and that everything is neat and orderly.

Even more crucial are the benefits that will accrue from neatness. Everybody will know where things are. Information will be accessible. And a neat office reinforces the pressure on people to keep things simple and to finish each task as it comes up rather than putting it on a "look-at-later" mountain.

FIGURE 9.2. Three steps to a more efficient office.

9.3. THE ONE-IS-BEST CAMPAIGN

The one-is-best campaign is a means of streamlining operations and facilitating management. Basically, it is a way of avoiding redundancy in that it strips away the non-essentials and enforces essentials. (See Figure 9.3.)

There are all kinds of "ones" involved here. Some of the better known are

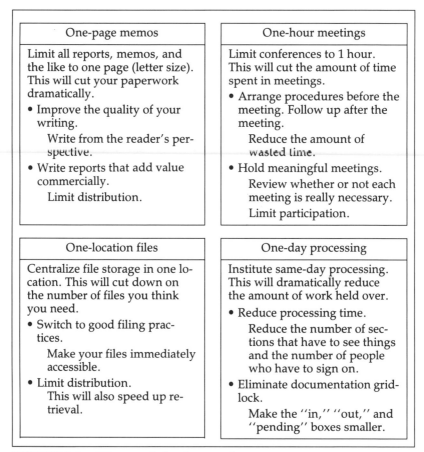

One-page memos	One-hour meetings

Limit all reports, memos, and the like to one page (letter size). This will cut your paperwork dramatically.
• Improve the quality of your writing.
  Write from the reader's perspective.
• Write reports that add value commercially.
  Limit distribution.
	Limit conferences to 1 hour. This will cut the amount of time spent in meetings.
	• Arrange procedures before the meeting. Follow up after the meeting.
	  Reduce the amount of wasted time.
	• Hold meaningful meetings.
	  Review whether or not each meeting is really necessary.
	  Limit participation.

One-location files	**One-day processing**

Centralize file storage in one location. This will cut down on the number of files you think you need.
• Switch to good filing practices.
  Make your files immediately accessible.
• Limit distribution.
  This will also speed up retrieval.
	Institute same-day processing. This will dramatically reduce the amount of work held over.
	• Reduce processing time.
	  Reduce the number of sections that have to see things and the number of people who have to sign on.
	• Eliminate documentation gridlock.
	  Make the "in," "out," and "pending" boxes smaller.

FIGURE 9.3. The one-is-best campaign.

- one location (keeping each file in only one location)
- one-day processing
- one-file projects (file consolidation)
- one-hour meetings (limiting conferences to 1 hour)
- one-page memos
- one-minute telephone calls
- one-tool work (limiting people to, at most, one of each tool)
- one-copy filing (keeping only the original of each document, and not making a lot of photocopies)

One-day processing, for example, means processing each day's work that day. This is a basic rule that you ignore at your peril, because work that is not done has a way of piling up, taking longer and longer while you try to remember what was involved, and filling up your files with dead backlog.

Professors Aida and Umezawa of Kyoto University are among some of the best organizers around. As mentioned earlier, Aida, for example, picks up his mail when he goes past the department office in the morning, and he already has it divided into "must look at" and "throw away" by the time he gets to his office. That way, he is ready to read the essential mail and to take care of his correspondence the first thing in the morning. Because he does this 5S activity (sorting his mail) while he is walking, he does not need to set aside a special time for it.

9.4. FILING

Perhaps the most urgent needs in office 5S activities are cleaning out and organizing your paperwork. Devise ways to enable anybody to find anything in 30 seconds. This may mean getting rid of envelopes and switching to binders with the pertinent information shown clearly on the spine and perhaps even color coded for faster identification. Go through and weed out things that you do not need anymore, and keep doing this on a regular basis. Once you have things in binders, introduce the principle that such binders are community property, because that then logically leads to keeping them in just one convenient place and eliminates the temptation for everyone to make his or her own photocopies of everything. (See Figure 9.4.)

Cleaning out and organizing your filing system will have to depend on categorization and systemization. Binders should, for example, all be vertical rather than laid on their sides. You should not have to move five binders to get at the one you want. They should be numbered consecutively on their spines and kept in order (including some way so that it is immediately obvious if they are out of order or if one is missing). (See Figure 9.5 and Photos 9.1 through 9.3.)

It is also a good idea to use fairly thin binders, because that also makes things easier to find. You might think it saves space to consolidate binders into heavy tomes, but you will end up losing more in time than you save in space. If you want to save space, throw things out.

These filing principles also apply to your computer floppy disks. You need to take good care of the floppies—not just in the sense of keeping them from getting bent, but in the larger sense of standardizing programs and formats and enabling everyone to understand what is where.

9.5. DESK DRAWERS

In most offices, people have many tools just put in a jumble in their desk drawers. People typically have several pens, for example, and still have trouble finding one when they need it. That is why it is important to limit people to one of each—one pencil, one black pen, one red pen, etc. One way to do this, of course, is to devise storage holders that only have room for one of each.

There are also many things such as punches, staplers, and the like that people use infrequently and do not need to have cluttering their desk drawers. Office 5S activities are an important issue at every company, and every office can benefit from an active program.

Purpose of filing

Facilitate the work by organizing the files so that you can find the information you need when you need it, and throwing out the files you do not need.

Thirty-second retrieval

1. Clearly specify where each file and document belongs. Mark each shelf and cabinet to show what is there. Speed up processing by enabling people to get at the information they need right away.

2. Make it possible for everyone to access and use the information. Organize your files by section, department, division, and the like. Do not create a situation in which only one person knows what is there and only one person has access to the files.

3. Only save the documents and files you really need. Draw up standards and criteria for what will be saved and what will be discarded. Avoid complex systems and dead space. Avoid wasted space and inefficient processing.

Filing checklist

1. Does this document have to be filed?

2. Are all the sheets and appendices there?

3. Are there any extraneous materials there that should not be there?

4. Have all the documents been dated with both date of receipt and date of processing?

5. Are the key words and titles clear?

6. Are the file numbers and "store to" dates clear?

Files in use

- Designate someone to be responsible for the files in shared use (blueprints, ledgers, contracts, etc.) so they do not get lost or misplaced. Require that everyone wanting to check out a file go through that person or go through other procedures. That way you will always know where everything is.

- Label each file with the name of the person responsible for it.

File name:
Custodian:

Classification

1. By client: Group your files by client name (e.g., suppliers and customers)

2. By subject: Group your files by content (e.g., inventory files and monthly total files)

3. By document type: Group your files by document type (e.g., approvals and regulations)

4. By title: Group your files by title (e.g., estimates, orders, and bills)

5. By project: Group your files by project (e.g., plant construction and personnel)

File category

FIGURE 9.4. Filing.

FIGURE 9.5.   The ultimate test.

PHOTO 9.1.   The diagonal line tells you they are in order.

PHOTO 9.2. The individual's tools.

SUMMARY

- Office 5S activities should concentrate first on the office's central functions. Because the office is a place where large numbers of people generate large volumes of paperwork and information, this means focusing on how these people process information and paperwork. This looks deceptively

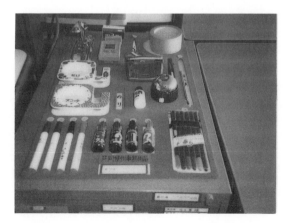

PHOTO 9.3. Things that everyone uses.

easy, but it is essential that you take the time to get it right and to instill good habits. A quick once-over is a waste of time.

- The typical office generates reams of unnecessary paperwork every day. Just storing this is a job in itself. And because so much of the work is done by individuals exercising individual discretion and initiative, it very often happens that the individual is the only one who understands a given job—which works against standardization and organization. The office sets the standards for the company. It determines most people's first impressions of the company—not only the people who see the physical office itself, but those who deal with you over the phone or get your paperwork.

- The increasing use of computers and other office equipment has created new areas demanding 5S treatment. Floppy disks are now an important filing system, but they have to be filed themselves.

- The office is management's home ground. If you cannot implement the 5S's in the office, how can you expect to do any better in the factory? Just as management has to take the initiative in instituting the 5S's companywide, the 5S effort has to start in the office.

Chapter 10

Getting the Most Out
of the 5S's

10.1. DRAWING UP A CAMPAIGN

Activity Stratification

It is intrinsic to 5S activities that the more you do them, the
more problems you discover and the more difficult it seems to
be just to maintain the status quo. It is all very well and good
for a leader to be out in front, but it is disastrous if you turn
around and find that nobody is following you, or if you find
that things are good only for the instant that you are watching
and then immediately fall apart again, or if it looks like you
are constantly having to run around putting out fires. In such
a situation, it is only natural that people should want to call it
quits. But you do not need to get into that kind of a situation.
You should not have to keep putting out fires. Your job is fire
prevention.

In promoting 5S activities, the important thing is to do them one at a time and to do them thoroughly. Even the little things have to be done thoroughly if they are to make any meaningful impact. Very broadly speaking, 5S activities can be stratified as follows:

1. Make a decision and implement it (e.g., the decision to get rid of everything you do not need, the decision to have a major housecleaning, and the decision to have 3-minute clean-up periods).
2. Make tools and use them (e.g., special shelves and stands for things, instructional labels, and placement figures).
3. Do things that demand *kaizen* and improvements as prerequisites (e.g., covers to prevent filings from scattering and measures to prevent leakage).
4. Do things that require help from other departments (e.g., fixing defective machinery, changing the layout, and preventing oil leakage).

The first two categories demand lots of participation, and you need to involve everyone if they are to have any lasting impact. This is also when backsliding is most common, and you need constant reminders, supervision, and other things to keep them uppermost in everyone's mind. By contrast, the second two categories need lots of ideas. You need to consider not only what has to be done, but when it might be done and how much it might cost.

None of these things is easy. Yet each one has to be done, and that is why it is so important that you decide what the goals are and how they can be reached. Decide which of these things you can do by yourself and which ones you need help on. And try to set up some kind of a timetable.

Formulating and Implementing Basic Plans

Specifically, you need to formulate a 5S plan and then follow through on its implementation. (See Figure 10.1.)

The first thing is to set up your basic plan giving the timing

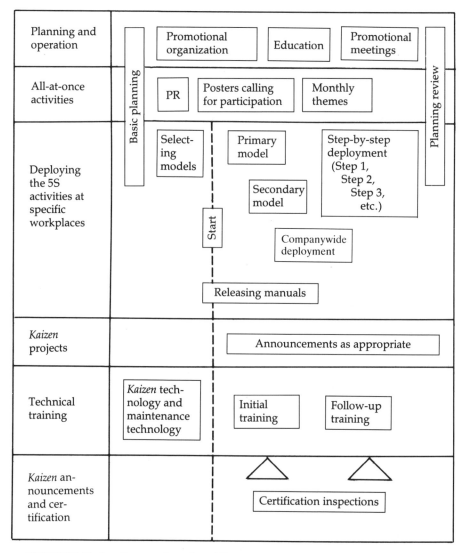

FIGURE 10.1. Promoting the 5S's.

on these things. This plan should be in very broad terms such as 1 year, 2 years, and so on, and you should be constantly reviewing both the timetable and what you are trying to do. In addition, the plan should also include provisions for conferences and reports whenever you review targets and whenever a goal is achieved. Do not restrict this to just a few people. Make a production out of the conference. Inviting other people to witness the success makes recognition all the better for the people who did the work.

Getting People To Realize the Need For An Organization

In the very early stages, you will have to spend a lot of time on putting an organization together and on slogans, posters, and other publicity. This educational effort is essential, and it should be repeated at regular intervals in the same way the results are announced at regular intervals. When all is said and done, it is most important that everybody be thinking along the same lines and in the same direction. Top management has to take the initiative in thinking about 5S education, and supervisors have to be the instructors leading the 5S effort on the workplace floor.

This is especially important in light of the many criticisms that are voiced about 5S in the initial stages, criticism such as, "The 5S's are not a way of eliminating waste, they *are* a waste—of time." "Surely we have better things to do with our time. What are we doing spending time on the 5S's?" "Here we go again with a big hoopla that is just going to peter out." Top management and the other supervisory personnel have to be believers, and they have to go at this with religious zeal. Getting off to a bad or weak start can endanger the entire program, and it is essential that you start strong and maintain the momentum.

Developing Kaizen Technology Education

The next step is to embark upon a program of *kaizen* technology education. This program should be supplemented with *kaizen* projects and opportunities for people to show off their accomplishments.

Workshop Deployment

In moving the 5S's to the actual workplace, there is no need to jump in all at once. Instead, you might want to designate model workplaces or model areas—both to develop experience and to show the other workplaces or areas what can be accomplished.

1. Moving ahead: In pushing ahead with the 5S activities, it is important to break this down into individual steps and to proceed step by step. You might even set goals and establish awards for each of the steps—a bronze prize for completion of the first step, silver for the second, gold for the third—to create greater incentives and to provide recognition at each stage.
2. What to do:
   * The first step should be a general housecleaning and an effort to get rid of everything you do not need. This is a prerequisite. Not only will a lot of other problems show up in the process, the other steps are impossible unless you have done this first.
   * Next is to create a cleaner workplace. Identify the causes of soiling and grime and correct them. In the first step, you cleaned up the workplace. This second step is to keep it that way. There are many workplace-specific issues involved here, and it is a good idea to form special project teams for some of the biggest ones. In addition to ensuring that the workplace and equipment are clean, feel free to change the layout and where things are kept. This is also a good chance to institute visual control policies. This is a big step, and it might be a good idea to break it down into a number of more manageable substeps.
   * The next step is to go into equipment 5S at the microlevel, improving where things are located and enhancing the

visual control mechanisms. Like the other steps, this step should also include training and practice to ensure that you have an orderly and disciplined workplace. As you go along, the 5S activities should be gradually expanded to more and more workplaces until it is a pervasive, companywide concern.

Although all of these steps are stages along the path to the same goal, it is important that each be fully implemented and that there be retrospectives and recognition every step of the way.

10.2. LEADERSHIP IN THE PROMOTIONAL CONFERENCE

Structuring the Promotional Conference

The promotional organization should be structured along the same vertical lines as the implementing organization. It should have top management at the top and should work down through the QC circles at the bottom. The head of each workplace should be the head of that workplace's promotional organization. In effect, it should parallel your management structure. (See Figure 10.2.)

Establishing the Promotional Conference

Once you have this worked out, the next step is actually to form your promotional conference with the people responsible for promoting the 5S activities (the production chiefs). This conference should be the highest policy-making body for 5S activities and should be charged with planning and implementation, setting goals, creating the structures needed to make everyone 5S-minded, and all of the other work of promoting 5S activities. It is imperative that these people also be willing to go the workplace and actually give instruction and advice on the 5S's.

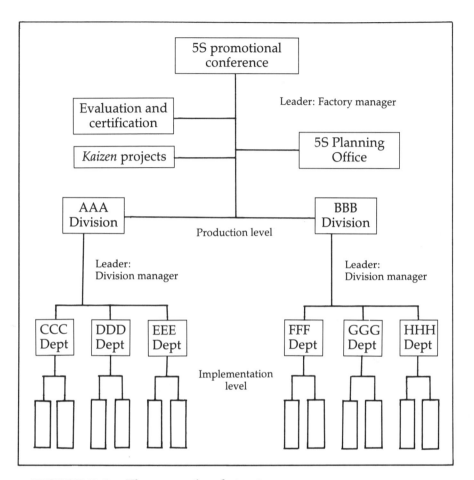

FIGURE 10.2.   The promotional structure.

As might be imagined, it is essential that all of these people be very strongly motivated and that they be able to motivate others. These are your leaders, and they have to believe in the cause that they are leading and to convert others to the faith. This is crucial, and you have to make sure that you get this right.

Evaluation and Planning

The evaluation and certification people are central to the operation's management. Because it is essential that this evaluation be done with authority, everyone should know who is doing the evaluation and they should be broadly acknowledged as the most capable people available.

The 5S Planning Office should be charged with formulating plans for implementing the 5S activities. As such, it should be working within the parameters set by the conference and should be looking at how these goals can best be achieved in each set of circumstances. Planning is very often criticized by the actual doers, but a good planning office should be able to come up with plans that are both reasonable and doable and that other people are inclined to follow. Much of this involves being able to break down the process into stages and to set manageable tasks and achievable goals for each stage. In addition, planning should include planning for recognition when these goals are met.

Kaizen Projects

Kaizen projects can be formulated as the need arises. When there are specific issues that need to be addressed—such as improving the dust collection equipment—teams can be formed including both the shop people and the technical people to work on them. If this is done, each team will have specific goals and specific timetables, and there will not be any sense of needless effort.

Management's Role

The top-management personnel should be involved at each level and should head the effort at that level. These people need to talk with everyone on what they want and need to create a 5S vision that everyone can adhere to. It is a good idea to have meetings once or twice a month to follow up and to discuss what kinds of support are needed for attaining priority goals.

This will be a constant process, demanding that the people responsible for implementing the 5S activities make innumerable policy decisions, and it is essential that they take their responsibilities seriously. The decision to throw something out, for example, is not an easy one, and the people need to be so clear in their own minds about what is involved that they can win other people over to their point of view. People lower down in the organization are very astute, very critical observers, and everything you do will have an impact on the 5S activities' success or failure.

10.3. KEEPING RECORDS

It is important to keep records, not only of decisions made, but also of the problems encountered, what was done, and what resulted. All too often, people make the improvements and then get used to the new way things are and forget the ''before'' situation. It is important that people have a sense of history—including the feeling that they are making history.

Photographs

Photographs are one excellent way of keeping records. There should be pictures of the situation before you start, pictures of people doing things, and pictures of what they did. There should be both full-view pictures of the shop and close-up pictures of specific parts and places. These photographs not only provide points of reference for the people involved, they can also be used to publicize the progress at companywide 5S meetings and to show outside experts.

The "P" Mark

Use a bright red or yellow to put P's on problem places and places that need attention. You might even have special days when this is done or special teams to do it, and the P's should serve as a vivid reminder of how much remains to be done. Conversely, a workplace with no P's is either a workplace that has not been checked yet or a workplace that has already done as much as could be done—and the difference will be immediately obvious to any observer.

Quantification

It is very important that you find ways to quantify what you are doing and the progress that you have made. This can be as simple as before-and-after comparisons to measure the amount of oil no longer lost to leakage or the amount of filings no longer being swept up. Use your imagination and be creative here in how you want to quantify these things to make the results more understandable. Aside from giving you a better handle on what is being done, numbers have a persuasiveness of their own that can be used to convince the skeptics.

Museum Rooms

As a last resort, you can keep some of the old tools and equipment in a special museum room—a display of how primitive things used to be. This is very difficult to do, but such displays have much more impact than any amount of photographs or statistics.

10.4. *KAIZEN* AND TECHNICAL TRAINING

The 5S activities are all directed at eliminating waste and effecting *kaizen* in the workplace. Even at first, there will seem to be lots of things to do. And as you go on, you will notice that there are more and more things to do. Yet if you approach these problems one by one, they are not insurmountable.

The important thing is how you implement kaizen. Although much of the 5S activities are aimed at maintaining things as they are and preventing backsliding, that assumes you are already at a desirable level. That is why there are other 5S aspects that are intended to help you get to the point at which maintaining the status quo can be a goal. The *kaizen* techniques are also important here.

With so many problems and so many *kaizen* ideas to choose from, what should you do? 5S has come a long way from the days when it was perceived as primarily a housecleaning operation. The 5S's are today aimed not just at cleaning, but at cleaning as a way of identifying problems and enabling people to do the necessary *kaizen*. Initiative is the key.

Doing it yourself. In promoting the 5S activities, there is great emphasis on having people do things themselves and devising their own solutions. Yet this should not translate into a knee-jerk desire to discard anything that anyone else has made or done. Instead, you should improve on the other people's efforts. True progress is achieved not in one great leap, but in small increments, every step building upon every other step until you finally get where you want to go. And each step is more difficult than the ones before.

Progress means discovering new problems. Much of the training and education that is provided today is training in management and control technology, and very little of it enables people to implement new *kaizen* ideas. This is a major shortcoming. It is essential in the 5S activities that you train people to be able to devise and implement their own solutions. Progress that is not self-sustaining—progress that always has to rely upon outside help—is not real progress. That is why it is important that your people know, for example, how to do welding even if it is not part of their job description. They need to study mechanical principles and to have a good theoretical and practical grasp of how the equipment that they use works. They need to study maintenance techniques. And oddly enough, the more problems they are capable of solving, the more problems they will spot.

This should also include sectionwide or companywide meetings where people can announce their results. Not only does this provide incentive, the exchange of ideas and information is often just what you need to keep everybody fresh.

10.5. DIAGNOSIS AND EVALUATION

As with so many other things, it is very easy to get into a rut with 5S activities—particularly because they demand constant, everyday attention to routine details. At the same time, because the individual tasks appear minor even though they have great cumulative impact, it is easy to think that you can put them off. Everybody is busy, and it is difficult to make alert 5S activities a part of the daily routine. Workplace evaluations and other means are needed to keep everyone abreast of what is happening and to spot problems before they develop into major complications. In essence, you need to devise ways that will get everybody competing in a friendly but no less intense manner. Your diagnostic tools are the key.

Diagnosis

From the very beginning, you need diagnostic methods that will tell you how far you have come. One of the most common—the grade diagnostic method—is shown in Figure 10.3. When the target workplace or project is viewed against set criteria and standards, it should be possible to tell how much progress has been made and to grade the effort. There can be either self-evaluation by the people who are doing the activity or an evaluation by outside (including in-house) experts.

In this example, the process is divided into three steps,

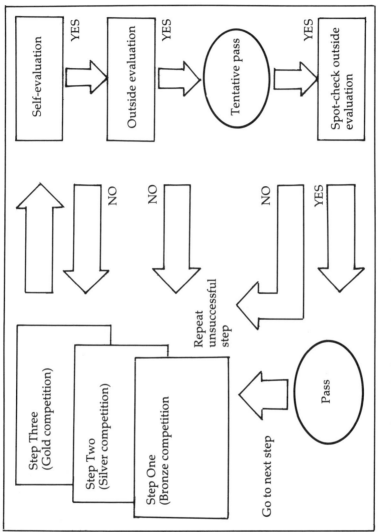

FIGURE 10.3. The grade diagnostic method.

with self-evaluations at each step of the way and with successful completion enabling the team to move on to the next step. At the same time, there are spot-check outside evaluations, and it is only when the team has successfully passed these expert evaluations that it can be truly said to have passed the step. Although this has been mentioned before, dividing the process into manageable, doable steps like this and providing recognition each step of the way enhances the sense of accomplishment.

Competitions

A single team working in isolation soon gets tired—even if it is evaluated and recognized by management. Team competitions are therefore a useful way to sustain interest and to drive people to even greater peaks of excellence. The analogy with sports is obvious, and there are two main ways that this is done.

Leagues

Competitions are not much fun unless everyone is at basically the same level and everyone has a chance of winning. Thus, it is that many companies create leagues. There could be, for example, the 1987 league of all the workplaces that started 5S activities in 1987. Within the league, the individual competitions could be scored and then league titles determined by the simple numbers of wins and losses, by the total margin of victory (such that a very resounding win might be worth as much as two or even three narrow wins), or by some other formula.

Tournaments

In a tournament, everyone competes at the first level, the winners of the first-level competition compete at the second level, and so on until you get to the grand championship playoffs. This is, for example, the practice at the Wimbledon Tennis

Championships, except that you would not have any "seeded" teams. And, of course, you might want to have lower-level playoffs between the losers so that the teams that are eliminated early do not lose interest.

Whichever method is chosen, it is important that the scoring and other criteria be clear from the very beginning and that everyone not only be familiar with the rulebook, but accept its validity—because otherwise they are going to think that the system is arbitrary and that they do not have a chance at winning. The whole point of competitions is to motivate people to do their best, and anything that does not contribute to this is counterproductive.

Evaluation Criteria

Evaluation criteria are obviously needed in determining winners and losers and in deciding whether or not a team is ready to go on to the next stage. Table 10.1 is one such possibility that details the various items at each of the stages. In addition, Table 10.2 shows a checklist of the most important factors at the introductory stage.

It is not enough that the judges know these criteria, they have to be explained to and accepted by everyone. Everyone has to be able to do the self-evaluations and to see where they need more work. Simply leaving people to their own devices is not enough.

Once the evaluation criteria have been determined, it is important that evaluations be clear-cut. In baseball, each pitch is either a strike or a ball. There is no "strikeish" or "ballish." You might call the two Pass (P) and Fail (F), Yes (Y) and No (N), or some other dichotomy of your choosing, but it is important that there just be two rankings, one at each end.

Patrols and cross-evaluation. Two other techniques that you can adopt to promote the 5S activities are patrols and cross-evaluation. Patrols can go around to the various workshops

TABLE 10.1. 5S evaluation criteria.

		Level 1	Level 2	Level 3	Level 4	Level 5
1	5S promotion at the workplace	Have 5S promotion chart and plans, and is working on 5S education.	5S promotion committee meets regularly and is aware of problems (including keeping minutes).	Committee plans implemented with full participation.	Problems explicated, plan drawn up for making improvements, and plan going according to schedule.	Results are visible to all, and all objectives are being met.
2	Cleaning (of main equipment)	Have cleaning plans with delineation of individual responsibilities and map, and education has reached everyone.	Cleaning of lubrication parts and around equipment completed.	Cleaning of peripheral equipment completed.	Cleaning of main equipment completed.	Able to detect problems in the making as well as abnormal noises, temperature levels, vibrations, etc.
3	Dealing with causes	Education completed and everyone able to identify causes of grime.	Have map of causes and plan for dealing with them	Implementation plan 50% or more completed.	Implementation plan 80% or more completed.	Working to modify (improve) equipment, and full plan implementation making it possible to do quick cleaning.
4	Hard-to-clean places	Education completed and everyone able to identify hard-to-clean places.	Have map of causes and plan for dealing with them	Implementation plan 50% or more completed.	Implementation plan 80% or more completed.	Able to improve cleaning equipment, covers, etc., and full plan implementation making it possible to do quick cleaning.

#	Item					
5	30-second put-away and get-out	Able to distinguish between necessary and unnecessary.	Have clearly designated places for everything.	Storage places clearly labeled.	Things put away for easy access.	Can access and put away in 30 seconds for better efficiency.
6	Safety	Know where to check equipment and what to check for.	Able to make all of the safety checks for all equipment.	Able to identify problems and formulate plans.	All safety plans implemented.	Safety educated and able to make safety improvements for a safer workplace.
7	Visual controls (1): Showing flow directions	Education completed and know how many are needed.	50–70% of pipes painted and labeled.	70–99% of pipes painted and labeled.	All pipes painted and labeled.	Have equipment ledger and map. Regular inspections to ensure work is error-free and safety is assured.
8	Visual controls (2): Valve instructions	Education completed and know how many of what kinds of labels are needed.	50–70% of valves labeled.	70–99% of valves labeled.	All valves labeled and check at least twice daily.	Have equipment ledger and map. Regular inspections to ensure work is error-free and safety is assured.
9	Visual controls (3): Wires and ropes	Education, including points on safety, completed and know how many of what there are.	All wires and ropes color coded.	All wires and ropes measured and cared for.	Have equipment ledger and care for wires and ropes when returned to inventory as well as when in use.	All wires and ropes taken care of so they are in top shape all the time.

(continued)

TABLE 10.1. 5S evaluation criteria (continued).

		Level 1	Level 2	Level 3	Level 4	Level 5
10	Visual controls (4): Fire-fighting equipment	Education completed and know how many of what there are.	70% clearly marked and people responsible designated.	100% clearly marked and people responsible designated.	Have equipment ledger and do regular inspections.	Have map and everyone knows how to use equipment. Able to rotate responsibilities, change markers, and maintain things in top shape.
11	Visual controls (5): Temperature labels	Education completed and know how many of what there are.	50–70% of equipment labeled.	70–99% of equipment labeled.	All equipment labeled and labels checked daily.	Have equipment ledger and check for label discoloration, etc. Improvements made and problems prevented.
12	Visual controls (6): Okay marks	Education completed, have action plan, and know what needs attention.	50–70% of equipment labeled.	70–99% of equipment labeled.	All equipment labeled.	Have equipment ledger, conduct regular inspections, and prevent problems.
13	Visual controls (7): Cooling fans	Education completed and places needing tape identified.	50–70% of places taped.	70–99% of places taped.	All places taped.	Have equipment ledger, check fans daily, and prevent problems.

TABLE 10.2. 5S evaluation checklist.

Category		Manual number	P/F
Floors	1 No oil or filings spilled on floors		
	2 No trash or parts on floors		
	3 No defectives strewn about		
	4 Floors are clean		
	5 No chipping or paint flaking on floors		
	6 No chipping or breaks in delineation lines		
Dollies & handlifts	7 Clear indications of who is responsible for each		
	8 All in good working condition		
	9 All wheels free of trash and filings		
	10 Clear indications where each one belongs		
Transit boxes	11 All in place as marked with right angles and straight lines		
	12 None at slant or higher than regulation		
	13 None broken		
	14 All free of trash and filings		
Equipment	15 All numbered and capacities indicated		
	16 No graffiti		
	17 Nothing put on equipment where it should not be		
	18 Process foolproofing devices on equipment		
	19 No non-essential labels or stickers		
	20 Danger marks affixed to all dangerous places		
Oil equipment	21 Oilers contain required amount of oil		
	22 Filters have no more than required number of drains		
	23 Pressure gauges have standard pressure indications		
Measurement equipment	24 None dirty or rusted		
	25 All put so metal parts do not bump up against each other		
	26 All have place, and all stored in proper place		
	27 None being used beyond inspection period		

(continued)

TABLE 10.2. 5S evaluation checklist (continued).

Category		Manual number	P/F
Lubrication	28 All intakes have labels indicating oil type		
	29 Oil tanks have cleaning and refill schedules posted		
	30 No leakage from pipes or gear boxes		
Misc. equip-ment	31 Valves all marked with open/shut directions		
	32 Bolts have "okay" marks as required		
	33 Fan and other belt covers labeled to show sizes and numbers		
	34 Motors (0.75kW or larger) have temperature labels)		
	35 Rotating parts have directional indications		
	36 Blades have inspection and replacement date labels		
	37 Dies and bits labeled with name (and code number)		
	38 Blades and tools have places and stored in proper places		
	39 Switches cleaned and oiled		
Meters	40 Pressure and power meters clean		
	41 Pressure and power meters labeled to show ranges		
Pipes and wires	42 No oil leakage from pipes or hydraulic units		
	43 Primary pipes color coded and have directional indicators		
	44 Wires bundled		
	45 Wires not in contact with other equipment		
	46 No breakage to tubes carrying bundles or wires		
	47 No loose or broken connectors		
Control panels	48 No grime, dust, or other foreign matter in panels		
	49 Every panel has its circuit diagram		
	50 All panels close tightly		
	51 No unnecessary holes in panels		
	52 No graffiti or unnecessary labels on panels		
	53 Power light lights up		

(continued)

TABLE 10.2. 5S evaluation checklist (continued).

Category		Manual number	P/F
Work-benches	54 Nothing that is not needed on any workbench		
	55 All workbenches clean with no breakage		
Notices	56 All notices clean and untorn		
	57 No out-of-date notices up		
	58 All notices have tops aligned and are parallel to sides		
Other areas (manage-ment)	59 5S responsibilities are clearly delineated at line level		
	60 Every operator knows his 5S responsibilities		

and point out problems. This is similar to "managing by walking around," but the patrol members do not even need to be management personnel. They simply need to know what to look for and have the authority to point out problems that need to be worked on. They simply need to know what questions to ask.

Cross-evaluations are a variation on this theme in that they involve having teams working on similar problems at similar levels (or teams that have recently completed a given level) offer advice to other teams. Although the idea of having a team one level higher do the evaluations, ask the questions, and offer the advice has immediacy; having teams at the same level do this has greater potential for the exchange of ideas and mutual education. Many companies, therefore, have teams at the same level look over each other's work as it is going forward and then have higher-level teams look at it just before the outside evaluation.

10.6. THE ROLE OF EVALUATORS

It is very important that the evaluations be conducted strictly. Everybody has worked hard getting ready for them, and it would never do for the evaluators to take a carefree or slipshod attitude to these evaluations. The evaluator who passes everyone because he or she wants to curry favor or who is not sure of himself or herself is worse than useless. The evaluations need to be done carefully and strictly by the book, looking at every detail and not missing anything. Although it is important to understand how much effort has gone into preparing for the evaluation, sympathy should not lead the evaluator to be soft on the grading. Rather, the evaluator should candidly remark on both the successes and the shortcomings, for awareness of the problems is the first step on the road to improvement.

The evaluator has to be very explicit about the problems that remain. Although this obviously requires extensive knowledge—much more than the people who are being graded—it also requires tact and sympathy. The evaluator's job is not easy. Some people have said that it is more difficult to be an evaluator than it is to undergo evaluation. Yet only when the evaluation is strict and fair will the people being graded have a true sense of accomplishment when they do pass.

SUMMARY

- There is no need to be afraid of 5S activities. They are not that difficult. The important thing is to get started, and sustaining the effort is the difficult part. People have all kinds of reasons why they cannot do 5S activities, why 5S activities are unnecessary, or why 5S activities will not have much impact anyway. Actual results are the best rebuttal to these excuses.

- It is important that top management take the lead and that everybody take part in 5S activities. Management attitudes are crucial. If management is not serious about 5S activities, nobody else will be either. But if management is determined to have a go at it and to succeed, this attitude will rub off on the other people and the whole company will be the better for it. Management sets the tone and, in large part, determines the campaign's success or failure.

- People will inevitably get tired and dirty when they clean up the workplace or when they make improvements on the equipment. This is difficult work. That is why it is important to break down the work into manageable steps and to have each step build upon the ones before it just like each stage of an assembly line adds to the ones before it to make a finished product.

- There can be no backsliding. Success has to be consolidated and achievements have to be recognized at each stage. At the same time, people have to realize that maintaining this success requires additional effort. One housecleaning is not enough. The workplace has to be kept neat every day of the week, every week of the year.

Index